GENOCIDE **&** PERSECUTION

South Africa

Titles in the Genocide and Persecution Series

GENOCIDE & PERSECUTION

I South Africa

Myra Immell
Book Editor

Frank Chalk
Consulting Editor

GREENHAVEN PRESS
A part of Gale, Cengage Learning

GALE
CENGAGE Learning·

Detroit • New York • San Francisco • New Haven, Conn • Waterville, Maine • London

Elizabeth Des Chenes, *Director, Content Strategy*
Cynthia Sanner, *Publisher*
Douglas Dentino, *Manager, New Product*

© 2014 Greenhaven Press, a part of Gale, Cengage Learning

WCN: 01-100-101

For more information, contact:
Greenhaven Press
27500 Drake Rd.
Farmington Hills, MI 48331-3535
Or you can visit our Internet site at gale.cengage.com.

For product information and technology assistance, contact us at:

Gale Customer Support, 1-800-877-4253
For permission to use material from this text or product, submit all requests online at www.cengage.com/permissions

Further permissions questions can be emailed to permissionrequest@cengage.com

Every effort is made to ensure that Greenhaven Press accurately reflects the original intent of the authors. Every effort has been made to trace the owners of copyrighted material.

Cover image © Charles O'Rear/Corbis.
Interior barbed wire artwork © f9photos, used under license from Shutterstock.com.

LIBRARY OF CONGRESS CATALOGING-IN-PUBLICATION DATA

South Africa (2014)
   South Africa / Myra Immell, Book Editor.
      pages cm. -- (Genocide and persecution)
   Includes bibliographical references and index.
   ISBN 978-0-7377-6894-7 (hardcover)
   1. Apartheid. 2. Political violence--South Africa. 3. Crimes against humanity--South Africa. 4. Human rights--South Africa. 5. South Africa--Politics and government--20th century. I. Immell, Myra. II. Title. III. Series: Genocide and persecution.
   DT779.952.S6525 2014
   968.06--dc23
                                                              2013037235

Printed in the United States of America
1 2 3 4 5 6 7 18 17 16 15 14

Contents

Chapter 1: Historical Background on Apartheid in South Africa

A South African diplomat who supports apartheid claims that it is a policy of self-preservation and argues that it is the best course of action for all South Africans, regardless of race.

An incarcerated antiapartheid activist relates what he and his prison mates learned about the 1976 Soweto uprising and describes his encounters with the young men arrested after the uprising.

Preface

> *"For the dead and the living, we must*
> *bear witness."*
>
> *Elie Wiesel, Nobel laureate and*
> *Holocaust survivor*

The histories of many nations are shaped by horrific events involving torture, violent repression, and systematic mass killings. The inhumanity of such events is difficult to comprehend, yet understanding why such events take place, what impact they have on society, and how they may be prevented in the future is vitally important. The Genocide and Persecution series provides readers with anthologies of previously published materials on acts of genocide, crimes against humanity, and other instances of extreme persecution, with an emphasis on events taking place in the twentieth and twenty-first centuries. The series offers essential historical background on these significant events in modern world history, presents the issues and controversies surrounding the events, and provides first-person narratives from people whose lives were altered by the events. By providing primary sources, as well as analysis of crucial issues, these volumes help develop critical-thinking skills and support global connections. In addition, the series directly addresses curriculum standards focused on informational text and literary nonfiction and explicitly promotes literacy in history and social studies.

Each Genocide and Persecution volume focuses on genocide, crimes against humanity, or severe persecution. Material from a variety of primary and secondary sources presents a multinational perspective on the event. Articles are carefully edited and introduced to provide context for readers. The series includes volumes on significant and widely studied events like the Holocaust, as well as events that are less often studied, such as the East Pakistan genocide in what is now Bangladesh. Some volumes focus on multiple events endured by a specific people, such as the Kurds, or multiple events enacted over time by a particular oppressor or in a particular location, such as the People's Republic of China.

Each volume is organized into three chapters. The first chapter provides readers with general background information and uses primary sources such as testimony from tribunals or international courts, documents or speeches from world leaders, and legislative text. The second chapter presents multinational perspectives on issues and controversies and addresses current implications or long-lasting effects of the event. Viewpoints explore such topics as root causes; outside interventions, if any; the impact on the targeted group and the region; and the contentious issues that arose in the aftermath. The third chapter presents first-person narratives from affected people, including survivors, family members of victims, perpetrators, officials, aid workers, and other witnesses.

In addition, numerous features are included in each volume of Genocide and Persecution:

- An annotated **table of contents** provides a brief summary of each essay in the volume.
- A **foreword** gives important background information on the recognition, definition, and study of genocide in recent history and examines current efforts focused on the prevention of future atrocities.
- A **chronology** offers important dates leading up to, during, and following the event.
- **Primary sources**—including historical newspaper accounts, testimony, and personal narratives—are among the varied selections in the anthology.
- **Illustrations**—including a world map, photographs, charts, graphs, statistics, and tables—are closely tied

to the text and chosen to help readers understand key points or concepts.

- **Sidebars**—including biographies of key figures and overviews of earlier or related historical events—offer additional content.
- **Pedagogical features**—including analytical exercises, writing prompts, and group activities—introduce each chapter and help reinforce the material. These features promote proficiency in writing, speaking, and listening skills and literacy in history and social studies.
- A **glossary** defines key terms, as needed.
- An annotated list of international **organizations to contact** presents sources of additional information on the volume topic.
- A **list of primary source documents** provides an annotated list of reports, treaties, resolutions, and judicial decisions related to the volume topic.
- A **for further research** section offers a bibliography of books, periodical articles, and Internet sources and an annotated section of other items such as films and websites.
- A comprehensive subject **index** provides access to key people, places, events, and subjects cited in the text.

The Genocide and Persecution series illuminates atrocities that cannot and should not be forgotten. By delving deeply into these events from a variety of perspectives, students and other readers are provided with the information they need to think critically about the past and its implications for the future.

to the text and chosen to help readers understand key points or concepts.

- **Sidebars**—including biographies of key figures and overviews of earlier or related historical events—offer additional content.
- **Pedagogical features**—including analytical exercises, writing prompts, and group activities—introduce each chapter and help reinforce the material. These features promote proficiency in writing, speaking, and listening skills and literacy in history and social studies.
- A **glossary** defines key terms, as needed.
- An annotated list of international **organizations to contact** presents sources of additional information on the volume topic.
- A **list of primary source documents** provides an annotated list of reports, treaties, resolutions, and judicial decisions related to the volume topic.
- A **for further research** section offers a bibliography of books, periodical articles, and Internet sources and an annotated section of other items such as films and websites.
- A comprehensive subject **index** provides access to key people, places, events, and subjects cited in the text.

The Genocide and Persecution series illuminates atrocities that cannot and should not be forgotten. By delving deeply into these events from a variety of perspectives, students and other readers are provided with the information they need to think critically about the past and its implications for the future.

Foreword

The term *genocide* often appears in news stories and other literature. It is not widely known, however, that the core meaning of the term comes from a legal definition, and the concept became part of international criminal law only in 1951 when the United Nations Convention on the Prevention and Punishment of the Crime of Genocide came into force. The word *genocide* appeared in print for the first time in 1944 when Raphael Lemkin, a Polish Jewish refugee from Adolf Hitler's World War II invasion of Eastern Europe, invented the term and explored its meaning in his pioneering book *Axis Rule in Occupied Europe*.

Humanity's Recognition of Genocide and Persecution

Lemkin understood that throughout the history of the human race there have always been leaders who thought they could solve their problems not only through victory in war, but also by destroying entire national, ethnic, racial, or religious groups. Such annihilations of entire groups, in Lemkin's view, deprive the world of the very cultural diversity and richness in languages, traditions, values, and practices that distinguish the human race from all other life on earth. Genocide is not only unjust, it threatens the very existence and progress of human civilization, in Lemkin's eyes.

Looking to the past, Lemkin understood that the prevailing coarseness and brutality of earlier human societies and the lower value placed on human life obscured the existence of genocide. Sacrifice and exploitation, as well as torture and public execution, had been common at different times in history. Looking toward a more humane future, Lemkin asserted the need to punish—and when possible prevent—a crime for which there had been no name until he invented it.

Legal Definitions of Genocide

On December 9, 1948, the United Nations adopted its Convention on the Prevention and Punishment of the Crime of Genocide (UNGC). Under Article II, genocide:

> means any of the following acts committed with intent to destroy, in whole or in part, a national, ethnical, racial or religious group, as such:
>
> (a) Killing members of the group;
>
> (b) Causing serious bodily or mental harm to members of the group;
>
> (c) Deliberately inflicting on the group conditions of life calculated to bring about its physical destruction in whole or in part;
>
> (d) Imposing measures intended to prevent births within the group;
>
> (e) Forcibly transferring children of the group to another group.

Article III of the convention defines the elements of the crime of genocide, making punishable:

> (a) Genocide;
>
> (b) Conspiracy to commit genocide;
>
> (c) Direct and public incitement to commit genocide;
>
> (d) Attempt to commit genocide;
>
> (e) Complicity in genocide.

After intense debate, the architects of the convention excluded acts committed with intent to destroy social, political, and economic groups from the definition of genocide. Thus, attempts to destroy whole social classes—the physically and mentally challenged, and homosexuals, for example—are not acts of genocide under the terms of the UNGC. These groups achieved a belated but very significant measure of protection under international criminal law in the Rome Statute of the International Criminal

Court, adopted at a conference on July 17, 1998, and entered into force on July 1, 2002.

The Rome Statute defined a crime against humanity in the following way:

> any of the following acts when committed as part of a widespread and systematic attack directed against any civilian population:
>
> (a) Murder;
>
> (b) Extermination;
>
> (c) Enslavement;
>
> (d) Deportation or forcible transfer of population;
>
> (e) Imprisonment or other severe deprivation of physical liberty in violation of fundamental rules of international law;
>
> (f) Torture;
>
> (g) Rape, sexual slavery, enforced prostitution, forced pregnancy, enforced sterilization, or any other form of sexual violence of comparable gravity;
>
> (h) Persecution against any identifiable group or collectivity on political, racial, national, ethnic, cultural, religious, gender . . . or other grounds that are universally recognized as impermissible under international law, in connection with any act referred to in this paragraph or any crime within the jurisdiction of this Court;
>
> (i) Enforced disappearance of persons;
>
> (j) The crime of apartheid;
>
> (k) Other inhumane acts of a similar character intentionally causing great suffering, or serious injury to body or to mental or physical health.

Although genocide is often ranked as "the crime of crimes," in practice prosecutors find it much easier to convict perpetrators of crimes against humanity rather than genocide under domestic laws. However, while Article I of the UNGC declares that countries adhering to the UNGC recognize genocide as "a crime under international law which they undertake to prevent and to punish," the Rome Statute provides no comparable international mechanism for the prosecution of crimes against humanity. A treaty would help individual countries and international institutions introduce measures to prevent crimes against humanity, as well as open more avenues to the domestic and international prosecution of war criminals.

The Evolving Laws of Genocide

In the aftermath of the serious crimes committed against civilians in the former Yugoslavia since 1991 and the Rwanda genocide of 1994, the United Nations Security Council created special international courts to bring the alleged perpetrators of these events to justice. While the UNGC stands as the standard definition of genocide in law, the new courts contributed significantly to today's nuanced meaning of genocide, crimes against humanity, ethnic cleansing, and serious war crimes in international criminal law.

Also helping to shape contemporary interpretations of such mass atrocity crimes are the special and mixed courts for Sierra Leone, Cambodia, Lebanon, and Iraq, which may be the last of their type in light of the creation of the International Criminal Court (ICC), with its broad jurisdiction over mass atrocity crimes in all countries that adhere to the Rome Statute of the ICC. The Yugoslavia and Rwanda tribunals have already clarified the law of genocide, ruling that rape can be prosecuted as a weapon in committing genocide, evidence of intent can be absent when convicting low-level perpetrators of genocide, and public incitement to commit genocide is a crime even if genocide does not immediately follow the incitement.

Several current controversies about genocide are worth noting and will require more research in the future:

1. Dictators accused of committing genocide or persecution may hold onto power more tightly for fear of becoming

vulnerable to prosecution after they step down. Therefore, do threats of international indictments of these alleged perpetrators actually delay transfers of power to more representative rulers, thereby causing needless suffering?

2. Would the large sum of money spent for international retributive justice be better spent on projects directly benefiting the survivors of genocide and persecution?

3. Can international courts render justice impartially or do they deliver only "victors' justice," that is the application of one set of rules to judge the vanquished and a different and laxer set of rules to judge the victors?

It is important to recognize that the law of genocide is constantly evolving, and scholars searching for the roots and early warning signs of genocide may prefer to use their own definitions of genocide in their work. While the UNGC stands as the standard definition of genocide in law, the debate over its interpretation and application will never end. The ultimate measure of the value of any definition of genocide is its utility for identifying the roots of genocide and preventing future genocides.

Motives for Genocide and Early Warning Signs

When identifying past cases of genocide, many scholars work with some version of the typology of motives published in 1990 by historian Frank Chalk and sociologist Kurt Jonassohn in their book *The History and Sociology of Genocide*. The authors identify the following four motives and acknowledge that they may overlap, or several lesser motives might also drive a perpetrator:

1. To eliminate a real or potential threat, as in Imperial Rome's decision to annihilate Carthage in 146 BC.

2. To spread terror among real or potential enemies, as in Genghis Khan's destruction of city-states and people who rebelled against the Mongols in the thirteenth century.

3. To acquire economic wealth, as in the case of the Massachusetts Puritans' annihilation of the native Pequot people in 1637.

4. To implement a belief, theory, or an ideology, as in the case of Germany's decision under Hitler and the Nazis to destroy completely the Jewish people of Europe from 1941 to 1945.

Although these motives represent differing goals, they share common early warning signs of genocide. A good example of genocide in recent times that could have been prevented through close attention to early warning signs was the genocide of 1994 inflicted on the people labeled as "Tutsi" in Rwanda. Between 1959 and 1963, the predominantly Hutu political parties in power stigmatized all Tutsi as members of a hostile racial group, violently forcing their leaders and many civilians into exile in neighboring countries through a series of assassinations and massacres. Despite systematic exclusion of Tutsi from service in the military, government security agencies, and public service, as well as systematic discrimination against them in higher education, hundreds of thousands of Tutsi did remain behind in Rwanda. Government-issued cards identified each Rwandan as Hutu or Tutsi.

A generation later, some Tutsi raised in refugee camps in Uganda and elsewhere joined together, first organizing politically and then militarily, to reclaim a place in their homeland. When the predominantly Tutsi Rwanda Patriotic Front invaded Rwanda from Uganda in October 1990, extremist Hutu political parties demonized all of Rwanda's Tutsi as traitors, ratcheting up hate propaganda through radio broadcasts on government-run Radio Rwanda and privately owned radio station RTLM. Within the print media, *Kangura* and other publications used vicious cartoons to further demonize Tutsi and to stigmatize any Hutu who dared advocate bringing Tutsi into the government. Massacres of dozens and later hundreds of Tutsi sprang up even as Rwandans prepared to elect a coalition government led by moderate political parties, and as the United Nations dispatched a small international military force led by Canadian general Roméo Dallaire to oversee the elections and political transition. Late in 1992, an international human rights organization's investigating team detected the hate propaganda campaign, verified systematic massacres of Tutsi, and warned the international community that Rwanda had already entered the early stages of genocide, to no avail. On April 6, 1994, Rwanda's genocidal killing accelerated at an alarming pace when someone shot down the airplane flying Rwandan president Juvenal Habyarimana home from peace talks in Arusha, Tanzania.

Hundreds of thousands of Tutsi civilians—including children, women, and the elderly—died horrible deaths because the world ignored the early warning signs of the genocide and refused to act. Prominent among those early warning signs were: 1) systematic, government-decreed discrimination against the Tutsi as members of a supposed racial group; 2) government-issued identity cards labeling every Tutsi as a member of a racial group; 3) hate propaganda casting all Tutsi as subversives and traitors; 4) organized assassinations and massacres targeting Tutsi; and 5) indoctrination of militias and special military units to believe that all Tutsi posed a genocidal threat to the existence of Hutu and would enslave Hutu if they ever again became the rulers of Rwanda.

Genocide Prevention and the Responsibility to Protect

The shock waves emanating from the Rwanda genocide forced world leaders at least to acknowledge in principle that the national sovereignty of offending nations cannot trump the responsibility of those governments to prevent the infliction of mass atrocities on their own people. When governments violate that obligation, the member states of the United Nations have a responsibility to get involved. Such involvement can take the form of, first, offering to help the local government change its ways through technical advice and development aid, and second—if the local government persists in assaulting its own people—initiating armed intervention to protect the civilians at risk. In 2005 the United Nations began to implement the Responsibility to Protect initiative, a framework of principles to guide the international community in preventing mass atrocities.

As in many real-world domains, theory and practice often diverge. Genocide and crimes against humanity are rooted in problems that produce failing states: poverty, poor education, extreme nationalism, lawlessness, dictatorship, and corruption. Implementing the principles of the Responsibility to Protect doctrine burdens intervening state leaders with the necessity of addressing each of those problems over a long period of time. And when those problems prove too intractable and complex to solve easily, the citizens of the intervening nations may lose patience, voting out the leader who initiated the intervention. Arguments based solely on humanitarian principles fail to overcome such concerns. What is needed to persuade political leaders to stop preventable mass atrocities are compelling arguments based on their own national interests.

Preventable mass atrocities threaten the national interests of all states in five specific ways:

1. Mass atrocities create conditions that engender widespread and concrete threats from terrorism, piracy, and other forms of lawlessness on the land and sea;

2. Mass atrocities facilitate the spread of warlordism, whose tentacles block affordable access to vital raw materials produced in the affected country and threaten the prosperity of all nations that depend on the consumption of these resources;

3. Mass atrocities trigger cascades of refugees and internally displaced populations that, combined with climate change and growing international air travel, will accelerate the worldwide incidence of lethal infectious diseases;

4. Mass atrocities spawn single-interest parties and political agendas that drown out more diverse political discourse in the countries where the atrocities take place and in the countries that host large numbers of refugees. Xenophobia and nationalist backlashes are the predictable consequences of government indifference to mass atrocities elsewhere that could have been prevented through early actions;

5. Mass atrocities foster the spread of national and transnational criminal networks trafficking in drugs, women, arms, contraband, and laundered money.

Alerting elected political representatives to the consequences of mass atrocities should be part of every student movement's agenda in the twenty-first century. Adam Smith, the great political economist and author of *The Wealth of Nations*, put it best when he wrote: "It is not from the benevolence of the butcher, the brewer, or the baker that we expect our dinner, but from their regard to their own interest." Self-interest is a powerful engine for good in the marketplace and can be an equally powerful motive and source of inspiration for state action to prevent genocide and mass persecution. In today's new global village, the lives we save may be our own.

Frank Chalk

Frank Chalk, who has a doctorate from the University of Wisconsin-Madison, is a professor of history and director of the Montreal Institute for Genocide and Human Rights Studies at Concordia University in Montreal, Canada. He is coauthor, with Kurt

Jonassohn, of The History and Sociology of Genocide *(1990); coauthor with General Roméo Dallaire, Kyle Matthews, Carla Barqueiro, and Simon Doyle of* Mobilizing the Will to Intervene: Leadership to Prevent Mass Atrocities *(2010); and associate editor of the three-volume Macmillan Reference USA* Encyclopedia of Genocide and Crimes Against Humanity *(2004). Chalk served as president of the International Association of Genocide Scholars from June 1999 to June 2001. His current research focuses on the use of radio and television broadcasting in the incitement and prevention of genocide, and domestic laws on genocide. For more information on genocide and examples of the experiences of people displaced by genocide and other human rights violations, interested readers can consult the websites of the Montreal Institute for Genocide and Human Rights Studies (http://migs.concordia.ca) and the Montreal Life Stories project (www.lifestoriesmontreal.ca).*

World Map

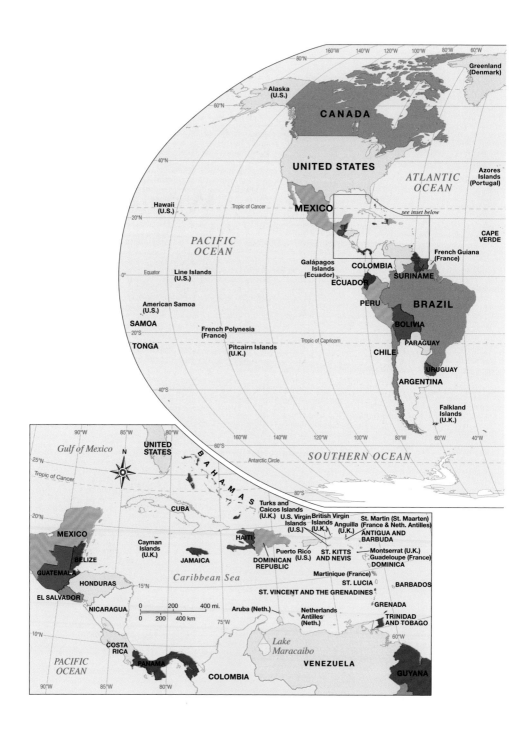

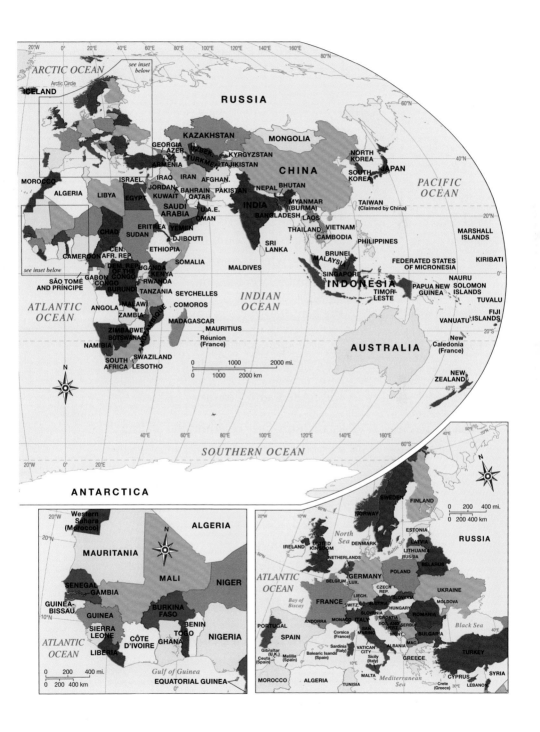

20°W   0°   20°E   40°E   60°E   80°E   100°E   120°E   140°E   160°E   80°N

ARCTIC OCEAN

see inset
below

Arctic Circle

ICELAND   60°N

RUSSIA

KAZAKHSTAN   MONGOLIA

GEORGIA   NORTH   40°N
AZER.   KYRGYZSTAN   KOREA
ARMENIA   TURKMEN. TAJIKISTAN   CHINA   SOUTH   JAPAN
MOROCCO   IRAQ IRAN AFGHAN.   KOREA   *PACIFIC*
                                                              OCEAN
ALGERIA LIBYA   ISRAEL   NEPAL BHUTAN
               JORDAN BAHRAIN PAKISTAN   TAIWAN   20°N
             KUWAIT QATAR   MYANMAR (Claimed by China)
         EGYPT SAUDI U.A.E.   INDIA   (BURMA)
                ARABIA OMAN   BANGLADESH LAOS   MARSHALL
            ERITREA YEMEN   THAILAND VIETNAM   ISLANDS
      CHAD SUDAN   DJIBOUTI   CAMBODIA
                                    SRI   PHILIPPINES
    CEN.   ETHIOPIA   LANKA   KIRIBATI
CAMEROON AFR. REP.   BRUNEI
see inset below UGANDA SOMALIA MALDIVES MALAYSIA FEDERATED STATES
        DEM. REP. KENYA   SINGAPORE OF MICRONESIA
SÃO TOMÉ GABON OF THE   NAURU   0°
AND PRÍNCIPE CONGO RWANDA   INDONESIA PAPUA NEW SOLOMON
         CONGO BURUNDI   TIMOR- GUINEA ISLANDS
ATLANTIC   TANZANIA SEYCHELLES *INDIAN* LESTE   TUVALU
OCEAN ANGOLA MALAWI COMOROS *OCEAN*   VANUATU FIJI
           ZAMBIA   ISLANDS
      ZIMBABWE   MADAGASCAR MAURITIUS   20°S
      BOTSWANA   Réunion
   NAMIBIA   (France)   AUSTRALIA New
                                                  Caledonia
      SWAZILAND   0   1000   2000 mi.   (France)
   SOUTH LESOTHO 0 1000 2000 km
   AFRICA   NEW   40°S
                                                   ZEALAND

N

40°E   60°E   80°E   100°E   120°E   140°E   160°E   60°S

SOUTHERN OCEAN

20°W   0°   20°E

ANTARCTICA

Western
Sahara   ALGERIA   SWEDEN FINLAND   RUSSIA
(Morocco)
                                NORWAY   ESTONIA
MAURITANIA   *North* IRELAND UNITED DENMARK LATVIA
                           Sea   KINGDOM   LITHUANIA
              MALI   NIGER   NETHERLANDS RUSSIA BELARUS
                           ATLANTIC   GERMANY POLAND
SENEGAL   *OCEAN* BELGIUM LUX. CZECH   UKRAINE
  GAMBIA   Bay of FRANCE LIECH. REP. SLOVAKIA MOLDOVA
GUINEA-   Biscay   SWITZ. AUSTRIA HUNGARY ROMANIA
BISSAU GUINEA BURKINA   ANDORRA MONACO SLOVENIA CROATIA SERBIA Black Sea
     SIERRA FASO   PORTUGAL   ITALY BOS. AND MONT. BULGARIA
     LEONE CÔTE BENIN   SPAIN Corsica HERZ.
          D'IVOIRE TOGO NIGERIA   (France) SAN ALBANIA
  LIBERIA   GHANA   Gibraltar   Sardinia MARINO MAC.   TURKEY
                             (U.K.) Melilla (Italy) VATICAN
ATLANTIC   Ceuta (Spain) Balearic Island CITY Sicily GREECE SYRIA
OCEAN   (Spain) (Spain) (Italy)   CYPRUS
0   200   400 mi.   MOROCCO ALGERIA MALTA Mediterranean (Greece) LEBANON
0 200 400 km EQUATORIAL GUINEA   TUNISIA Crete
Gulf of Guinea   Sea   (Greece)

0   200   400 mi.
0 200 400 km

17 |

Chronology

1910	The Union of South Africa is formed.
1911	The Mines and Works Act makes certain skilled jobs open to whites only.
1912	The South African Native National Congress (SANNC) is founded.
1913	The Native Lands Act allots 7.3 percent of South African land to black South Africans, who account for 80 percent of the country's population.
1914	The National Party is founded.
1923	SANNC changes its name to African National Congress (ANC).
1944	The ANC Youth League is formed.
1948	In a whites-only election, the National Party comes to power on an apartheid platform.
1950s	A great deal of apartheid legislation is passed, including the Population Registration Act, the Group Areas Act, the Bantu Homelands Act, the Bantu Education Act, and the Reservation of Separate Amenities Act.
1952	The ANC begins a Defiance Campaign, the first large-scale, multiracial political mobilization against apartheid laws under a common leadership.

1955	The Freedom Charter is adopted at the Congress of the People in Kliptown, a freehold area south of Johannesburg.
1956	The Treason Trial begins to try many key antiapartheid leaders and activists.
1960	Sixty-nine people are killed at Sharpeville during what comes to be known as the Sharpeville massacre; the white government bans the ANC.
1961	The Treason Trial ends; South Africa becomes a republic; the previously nonviolent ANC and the Pan Africanist Congress (PAC) go underground and form military wings that launch sabotage campaigns.
1962	The United Nations establishes the Special Committee Against Apartheid.
1963	ANC leaders, including Nelson Mandela, are put on trial in the Rivonia Trial.
1964	Nelson Mandela and other ANC leaders are imprisoned for life.
1969	Steve Biko starts the black consciousness movement and forms the South African Students' Organization (SASO).
1970	The Bantu Homelands Citizenship Act is passed, depriving Africans of their South African citizenship by making them automatic citizens of the homeland in which they live.

1976	The Soweto uprising begins when police open fire on thousands of students protesting the use of Afrikaans in schools.
1977	Steve Biko dies under suspicious circumstances while being held by the police.
1985	A disinvestment campaign gets underway; violence increases and leads to the declaration of a state of emergency in more than thirty magisterial districts.
1986	The state of emergency is extended to all of South Africa; the United States passes the Comprehensive Anti-Apartheid Act, which imposes trade and financial sanctions on South Africa.
1989	F.W. de Klerk becomes president of the National Party, then acting president of South Africa, and finally full president of South Africa; public facilities are desegregated; many ANC activists are released from prison.
1990	The ban on the ANC and other parties is lifted; Nelson Mandela is released from prison; President de Klerk announces plans to negotiate for majority rule.
1991	Negotiations get underway for majority rule; the last three apartheid laws are abolished; international sanctions are lifted.
1993	A multiracial, multiparty transitional government is approved.
1994	South Africa's first multiracial elections are held; Nelson Mandela is elected the

first black president of South Africa; remaining sanctions are lifted; South Africa once again takes a seat in the UN General Assembly.

1995   The Truth and Reconciliation Commission (TRC) is established.

1996   TRC hearings get underway; the South African parliament ratifies a new constitution.

1997   Nelson Mandela steps down as ANC president.

1998   The TRC issues the first five volumes of its final report, which labels apartheid a crime against humanity.

1999   Nelson Mandela retires, and Thabo Mbeki becomes president of South Africa.

2013   Nelson Mandela dies after a long illness. South Africa declares a national mourning period of ten days and holds a state funeral attended by more than ninety world leaders.

Historical Background on Apartheid in South Africa

Chapter Exercises

STATISTICS

South Africa

Total Area
1,219,090 sq km
World ranking: 25
Comparative area: slightly less than twice the size of Texas

Population
48,810,427
World ranking: 26
Urban population: 62%
Population below poverty line: 50%

Ethnic Groups
Black African 79%, white 9.6%, colored (mixed-race) 8.9%, Indian/Asian 2.5%

Languages
isiZulu (official) 23.82%, isiXhosa (official) 17.64%, Afrikaans (official) 13.35%, Sepedi (official) 9.39%, English (official) 8.2%, Setswana (official) 8.2%, Sesotho (official) 7.93%, Xitsonga (official) 4.44%, siSwati (official) 2.66%, Tshivenda (official) 2.28%, isiNdebele (official) 1.59%, other 0.5%

Religions
Protestant 36.6% (Zionist Christian 11.1%, Pentecostal/Charismatic 8.2%, Methodist 6.8%, Dutch Reformed 6.7%, Anglican 3.8%), Catholic 7.1%, Muslim 1.5%, other Christian 36%, other 2.3%, unspecified 1.4%, none 15.1%

Death Rate
17.23 deaths/1,000 population
Country comparison to the world: 1

Literacy
(total population)
86.4%

GDP
$555 billion
World ranking: 26

Labor Force
Agriculture 9%, industry 26%, services 65%

Source: *The World Factbook*. Washington, DC: Central Intelligence Agency, 2013. www.cia.gov.

1. Analyzing Statistics

Question 1: Examine the statistics on ethnic groups in South Africa. Which group or groups are primarily responsible for human rights violations in South Africa? Which group or groups have been major targets of persecution? Given the statistics, are these the groups you would expect to be the perpetrators and the victims? Why or why not?

Question 2: How does the gross domestic product (GDP) of South Africa compare with that of the rest of the world? What role did the economy and politics play in apartheid and black resistance to it?

Question 3: Consider the percentage of the total population that lives in urban areas and the percentage of the labor force in industry and services. Where would most jobs be? How might apartheid policy affect the way of life of non-whites and their ability to get a good education and earn a living?

2. Writing Prompt

Assume you are a member of an international human rights organization, such as Amnesty International or Human Rights Watch, and write a report on the human rights violations that occurred during the Sharpeville massacre and the Soweto uprising. Include a descriptive title for the report, a synopsis of what transpired, and any relevant background information. Identify who, in each case, committed the violations and who the victims were.

Apartheid in South Africa: An Overview

David Welsh

In the following viewpoint, South African political scientist David Welsh provides an overview of the history of apartheid in South Africa from its implementation by the National Party in 1948 until its demise in the 1990s. Welsh explains that from its inception, the goal of the apartheid policy was the maximum separation of whites and nonwhites. The intent was to reinforce racial inequality in areas where it was breaking down, limit the urbanization of Africans, and ensure complete political separation between whites and nonwhites. For more than forty years, nonwhites suffered increasing upheaval, duress, and hardship as a result of apartheid laws and restrictions that deprived them of their human and civil rights. Welsh is a scholar, human rights activist, and author of several books focused on South Africa, including The Rise and Fall of Apartheid: From Racial Domination to Majority Rule.

In 1948 the National Party, with the assistance of the small Afrikaner Party, which it subsequently absorbed, won a narrow election victory in South Africa and thereafter proceeded to implement the apartheid policy. . . .

David Welsh, "Apartheid," *New Encyclopedia of Africa*, vol. 1, John Middleton and Joseph C. Miller, eds. New York: Charles Scribner's Sons, 2008, pp. 88–91. Copyright © 2008 Cengage Learning.

From the policy's inception in 1948 it was made clear that while apartheid envisaged the maximum separation of whites and nonwhites, total separation, advocated by a few intellectuals, was not possible, due to the economic dependence of the economy on African, Coloured, and Indian labor. Instead, apartheid focused on two interlinked aims: reinforcing racial inequality wherever it was perceived to be breaking down (as in the labor market) and limiting the urbanization of Africans by freezing the number of permanently urbanized people and attempting as far as possible to ensure that migrant labor was used, as had long been the case in the mining industry. Policy also sought to ensure that white workers would be given additional protection in the labor market by means of "job reservation." African labor unions, while not prohibited, were not officially recognized, and strikes by African workers continued to be illegal. Legislation changed this situation, and during the 1980s African labor unions became a critical anti-apartheid force.

The Creation of Homelands

Apartheid prescribed total political separation between whites and nonwhites. [A] provision made in 1946 for limited communal parliamentary representation of Indians by whites (boycotted by the Indian community) was repealed, the rights of qualified Coloured males to vote on the common voters' roll in Cape Province were abolished in 1956 after a protracted constitutional crisis, and in 1959 the limited rights of Africans to parliamentary representation by whites were terminated. The central premise of apartheid was that blacks could enjoy political rights only in institutions created in the "homelands."

The homelands, previously called reserves, were the shrunken, fragmented remnants of land that had been historically occupied by black Africans. Under the terms of legislation passed in 1913 and 1936, they amounted to 13.7 percent of the country. Here, in the vision of apartheid's planners, African "nations," as the ethnolinguistic clusters were called, could enjoy evolving political rights and "develop along their own lines," while the homelands continued to serve their historic function as reservoirs of labor. Traditional chiefs were deemed to be the authentic leaders of the black African peoples, and beginning in the 1950s, energetic steps were taken to establish pyramids of so-called "Bantu Authorities" in the homelands. Policy postulated that Africans in the urban areas must remain linked to these authorities, and accordingly, efforts were made to create urban representatives of homeland chiefs. These, however, proved unsuccessful.

Focusing on Education Policy

A major focus of apartheid was the effort to gear education of blacks at all levels to the aims of policy. School education had been largely in the hands of missionary bodies under the aegis of provincial authorities. Under the Bantu Education Act of 1953 the central government assumed control, missionary-run schools were taken over, and a new curriculum was instituted. In the words of the legislation's sponsor, Hendrik F. Verwoerd (minister of native affairs, 1950–1958; prime minister, 1958–1966), who was also apartheid's principal planner and theoretician, the "Bantu must be guided to serve his community in all respects. There is no place for him in the European community above the level of certain forms of labor. Within his own community, however, all doors are open."

Education policy was ideologically inspired. Although the numbers of African children entering primary school rose substantially over time, the education they received was of poor quality. "Bantu Education" became a major political grievance: indeed, it was an educational issue, the attempt to force the teaching of certain subjects in higher grades through the medium of Afrikaans, that sparked the Soweto Uprising in mid-1976.

Apartheid was also enforced at the university level. Separate university colleges were established for Africans, as well as for Coloured and Indian students. These were mediocre institutions

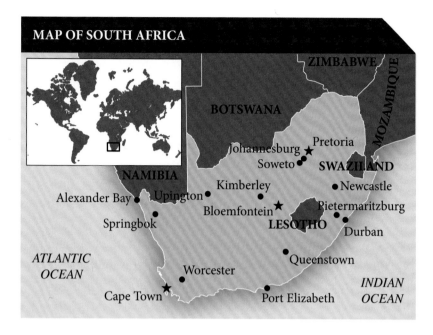

MAP OF SOUTH AFRICA

ZIMBABWE

MOZAMBIQUE

BOTSWANA

Johannesburg Pretoria
Soweto SWAZILAND

NAMIBIA

Kimberley Newcastle

Alexander Bay Upington
Bloemfontein Pietermaritzburg

Springbok LESOTHO Durban

ATLANTIC
OCEAN Queenstown

Worcester INDIAN
OCEAN

Cape Town Port Elizabeth

of low academic quality, whose students were kept under tight political control.

Effects of the Temporary Sojourner Principle

Vigorous efforts were made to reinvigorate the principle, upheld by successive governments since 1910, that urban Africans were "temporary sojourners." Beginning in the 1950s the pass laws, officially known as influx control, were drastically tightened and permanent rights of urban residence became hard to obtain. In 1960 the system was extended to women. Furthermore, freehold property rights were prohibited, and numerous black African communities that had enjoyed such rights in urban and rural areas (where they were termed *black spots*) were dispossessed. More than 3.5 million people were affected. Black African–owned businesses in urban areas were placed under severe restrictions that limited their capacity to expand. Deliberate measures were taken to ensure that the availability of family housing was limited, whereas, alternatively, huge hostels were constructed for single, male migrant laborers. The migrant labor system, favored by apartheid's planners because it supposedly limited permanent urbanization, played havoc with family life, breaking down functioning social and economic units in the rural areas and encouraging male migrants in the towns to start second families with urban women.

Prior to 1948 the Coloured and Indian groups (accounting, respectively, for 9% and 3% of the total population in 1992) were intermediate categories in the racial hierarchy; both, but especially the Indians, were discriminated against, particularly as residential segregation in terms of the Group Areas Act of 1950 was enforced. Between 1960 and 1984 an estimated 860,000 people, mostly Coloured and Indian, were forced to relocate if their houses or businesses were in areas zoned for occupation by other programs.

Resistance Against Apartheid

In 1959 a switch of emphasis in the ideological underpinning of apartheid took place. Whereas the maintenance of racial inequality was as rigidly enforced as previously, the National Party under Verwoerd now embarked upon "positive" apartheid, terming it "separate development." Legislation was enacted to give black Africans "full rights" to develop in the homelands, eight of which were designated on an ethnolinguistic basis. Verwoerd emphasized that whites would never cede or share power in the remainder of the country. Originally, policy held that political evolution of these embryonic states would stop short of sovereign independence, but this limitation was dropped after 1959.

By 1960 apartheid and the South African government's continuing control over Namibia had increasingly become the object of international censure. In his "Wind of Change" speech, delivered in Cape Town in 1960, British prime minister Harold Macmillan served notice that apartheid was an unacceptable doctrine. Shortly thereafter, on March 21, 1960, police opened fire on Africans in Sharpeville who were demonstrating against the pass laws, killing sixty-nine. The ensuing disturbances in different parts of the country were quelled, and the major black African political movements, the African National Congress (ANC) and the Pan-Africanist Congress [PAC], were banned. This was a landmark event in the increasing international isolation of the South African government.

After the banning of the ANC and the PAC, both opted to adopt violent methods of resistance. Nelson Mandela, a rising star in the ANC, joined the ANC's armed wing Umkhonto we Sizwe. He and eight others were arrested for sabotage and conspiracy to overthrow the government, and convicted in June 1964. All of the accused, but one, were sentenced to life imprisonment.

Verwoerd recognized that racial domination per se could no longer be justified in an increasingly hostile world in which, moreover, decolonization was proceeding apace. He attempted to appease criticism and to divert domestic black militancy by accelerating homeland political evolution. Ultimately four such homelands, Transkei (1976), Bophuthatswana (1977), Venda (1979), and Ciskei (1981), were granted independence, but in no case was it internationally recognized. Citizens of these states (whether they resided in them or not) were deprived of their South African citizenship. None was economically viable, and none, with the qualified exception of Bophuthatswana, succeeded in maintaining a semblance of democratic government. As the showpiece of apartheid they were a failure. . . .

An important component of apartheid was the vigorous use of security legislation to restrict opposition. Apart from proscribing organizations, individual activists were liable to be banned, detained without trial, and deprived of their passports, without recourse to judicial reviews. More serious breaches of the security laws were tried in the Supreme Court. Although many judges reflected conventional white supremacist attitudes, some did their best to find loopholes in the law that mitigated the consequences of apartheid. In political cases heard in the Supreme

Court the accused had the service of defense lawyers, often some of the leading barristers.

The Unraveling of Apartheid

During the 1970s and 1980s apartheid unravelled steadily. Predictions made by Verwoerd in the 1960s that by 1978 the townward flow of Africans from the homelands would cease were shown to be hopelessly inaccurate. Apartheid's planners had seriously underestimated the rate of increase of the African population, which between 1946 and 1991 had nearly quadrupled, from 7.7 million to more than 29 million. Influx control was unable to prevent black African urbanization, as economic conditions in the homelands deteriorated. Job reservation by race steadily fell away as the demand for skilled workers increased. Efforts to force industry to make do with less African labor or to decentralize factories to the borders of homelands proved costly failures.

P[ieter] W[illem] Botha (prime minister, 1978–1983; state president, 1983–1989) tried unsuccessfully to reinvigorate what was obviously a failing policy. He permitted black labor unions to participate in statutory industrial relations mechanisms, allowed urban Africans to acquire property in freehold, repealed legislation prohibiting interracial sex and marriage, and in 1986 abolished the pass laws. He acknowledged that the homelands could never support more than 40 percent of the black African population and accepted that those residents in the white-controlled areas would have to be politically accommodated in those areas. In 1986 he announced that a common South African citizenship would be restored to those homeland citizens who had been deprived of theirs. Effectively, this was a nail in apartheid's coffin: Its ideological basis, separate nations, had been abandoned.

Botha tried to co-opt the Coloured and Indian categories by means of the Tricameral Constitution of 1983. It was intended to accord political rights, in separate chambers of Parliament, in such a way as not to threaten or significantly dilute white hegemonic control. The exclusion of Africans, who were still deemed to have alternative channels of political expression, provoked a massive backlash. During 1985–1986 South Africa witnessed serious unrest that was curbed (partially) by the application of stringent emergency regulations. The mass mobilization of millions of people and the growing influence of the ANC persuaded President [F.W.] de Klerk that "South Africa had reached a point in its history that offered an opportunity to break out of the current impasse. . . ."

Apartheid had palpably failed in all respects, but by 1986 Botha had run out of reformist steam and until mid-1989 he and his party drifted rudderless. De Klerk came to the presidency at that time, and in his historic speech of February 2, 1990, he announced the lifting of the ban against the ANC and other proscribed organizations, the release of Nelson Mandela and other imprisoned leaders, and his intention of negotiating a democratic constitution. In subsequent years he repealed all apartheid legislation, and opened his party membership to all races.

Establishing Separate Communities for Different Races

M.A. Johnson

The following viewpoint reports that the white government of South Africa is moving forward with its policy of apartheid, or "apartness." Although separation of races is not new to South Africa, it is the first time it has been required by law. A key new element of the apartheid policy is the establishment of separate communities for different races, which apartheid supporters contend is necessary to keep the nonwhite majority from taking over the country. As a result of the new law, entire communities have been forced to leave their homes and relocate in government-specified areas for Africans, Indians, and Coloreds. The several million Africans living and working in the towns and cities have been hardest hit by this newest feature of apartheid. At the time this viewpoint was written, M.A. Johnson was a reporter for the Washington Post and Times Herald.

Here at the foot of the Dark Continent [Africa] the white man has chosen to stand firm against any attempt to give equality to men of darker skin.

Instead, government action has been initiated to deprive native Africans, Asians and persons of mixed blood of political, social and economic gains they acquired in earlier generations.

Today [in 1956] South Africa is moving steadily down the road of apartheid, which means separation of the country's races. There are no signs of turning back from the policy decreed by the nationalist government of Premier J.G. Strijdom, despite criticism from abroad and some dissension within South Africa.

Separation of the races in schools and almost all other places they might meet as equals has been traditional for most of the 300 years since the first white men settled in South Africa. It was enforced by custom. Now the law requires it.

Creating Separate Communities

The major new feature of Strijdom's apartheid policy is the establishment of separate communities for the different races. Most blacks and brown-skinned people who live in the white man's cities and towns are encouraged now to go back to communities of their own.

The great majority of whites favor racial segregation but there is some division over the wisdom of the new legislative program allowing little flexibility or hope of change.

In the view of its supporters, apartheid is necessary to prevent the whites—outnumbered 4 to 1 by the black and other colored races—from becoming submerged in a country the early white settlers developed.

There are nearly 3 million whites, who call themselves Europeans; some 9 million Africans, referred to here as natives or bantus; about 1¼ million persons of mixed native and other blood who are called "coloreds" and occupy a higher rung on the social ladder than the Africans, and 410,000 Indians who were brought here from Asia to labor in the sugar fields.

Four million of the Africans live a tribal existence in native reserves set aside exclusively for their use. These cover 12.9 per cent of the country. The Africans on the reserves still barter cattle for wives and heed advice of witch doctors.

But today the blare of American jazz mingles with the beat of native drums in even the most remote areas.

Some 2½ million Africans in towns and cities have tried to adjust themselves to the white man's way of life, mainly as menial laborers. These are the people most affected by apartheid. The remaining Africans work on the white man's farms.

The government has been classifying the racial groups into separate compartments with identity cards for each. For some persons of doubtful racial origin this has brought in different groups—the wife "colored" and the husband African, for instance—forcing separation and heartbreak. Colored persons, who often hold white collar jobs, stand to lose their social status and livelihood if classified as African.

Communities Are Uprooted

Whole communities have been uprooted and moved to areas designated for them.

Twenty thousand Indians in Johannesburg are to be moved to Lenasia, an undeveloped area 18 miles away where an all-Indian community is planned. For the 800 Indian shopkeepers in the city and their employees this means they will lose their businesses. They cater to the needs of the white economy and cannot survive by trading among themselves.

The government will reimburse them the value of their property, but not for the loss of their business.

The mass resettlement began last year when the first of 57,000 Africans in a Johannesburg slum area were sent to the new township of Meadowlands, 10 miles southwest of the city. Riots had been feared, so 2,000 police armed with Sten guns cordoned off the city's African section before the move. But the Africans accepted the resettlement peacefully and now seem to be content in their new township.

Apartheid Draws Opposing Views

A leading opponent of apartheid is the Anglican archbishop of Capetown, the Most Rev. Geoffrey Clayton. He says, "it is wrong to move people around like pawns, regardless of their wishes, to satisfy some ideology."

The *Johannesburg Star* has called the relocation of the Indians and the coloreds "mass callousness."

African native opponents of apartheid stated this view at a recent conference: "The situation in South Africa calls for co-operation and interdependence between the different races. . . . This would not constitute a threat to the survival of the white man in South Africa. Apartheid constitutes a threat to race relations."

On the other hand, the government's Minister of Native Affairs, Dr. H. F. Verwoerd, says: "Apartheid is the only hope for South Africa. Integration of the races is impossible if the white man wishes to continue in this country. It will only bring chaos and will lead eventually to black control of South Africa."

The government points to vast sums being spent to improve the housing, health services, education and general welfare of the Africans. It says it is making available to them greater opportunities for advancement to serve their own people.

The Sharpeville Massacre

Ambrose Reeves

*In the following viewpoint, Bishop Ambrose Reeves reports on the
1960 sequence of events that ended in the deaths of sixty-nine people and the injuring of 180 others in the South African township
of Sharpeville. The tragedy, the author explains, came about when
the police opened fire on a crowd of men, women, and children
resentful of South Africa's pass system. They had gathered expecting to hear an announcement about passes. Sharpeville, writes the
author, marked a watershed in South African affairs; it triggered
international denunciation of South Africa's apartheid policies
and led nonviolent antiapartheid movements to embrace a policy of armed resistance. Reeves served as the Anglican bishop of
Johannesburg, South Africa, from 1949–1961. In 1960, the same
year his book* Shooting at Sharpeville: The Agony of South Africa
was released, he was deported.

It was the events at [the South African township of] Sharpeville
on March 21, 1960, which shocked the world and which are
still remembered with shame by civilised men everywhere. Early
that morning a crowd of Africans estimated at between 5,000 and

7,000 marched through Sharpeville to the municipal offices at the entrance to the township. . . . Eventually this demonstration was dispersed by the police, using tear gas bombs and then a baton charge, some sixty police following them into the side streets. Stones were flung and one policeman was slightly injured. It was alleged that several shots were fired by Africans and that only then some policemen opened fire without an order from their officer to do so. Fortunately nobody was hurt. . . .

During the morning, news spread through the township that a statement concerning passes would be made by an important person at the police station later that day. The result was that many who had been concerned in the earlier demonstration drifted to the police station where they waited patiently for the expected announcement. And all the time the crowd grew. Reading from the police report on what subsequently happened the Prime Minister told the House of Assembly that evening that the police estimated that 20,000 people were in that crowd. This seems to have been a serious exaggeration. From photographs taken at the time it is doubtful if there were ever more than 5,000 present at any particular moment, though it may well be that more than this number were involved at one time or another as people were coming and going throughout the morning. . . .

The presence of this crowd seems to have caused a good deal of alarm to the police. So much so that at ten o'clock that morning a squadron of aircraft dived low over the crowd, presumably to intimidate them and encourage them to disperse. . . . The police claimed that the people in the crowd were shouting and brandishing weapons and the Prime Minister told the Assembly that the crowd was in a riotous and aggressive mood and stoned the police. There is no evidence to support this. On the contrary, while the crowd was noisy and excitable, singing and occasionally shouting slogans it was not a hostile crowd. Their purpose was not to fight the police but to show by their presence their hostility to the pass system, expecting that someone would make a statement about passes. Photographs taken that morning show clearly that this was no crowd spoiling for a fight with the police. Not only was the crowd unarmed, but a large proportion of those present were women and children. . . .

As the hours passed the increasing number of people in the crowd was matched by police reinforcements. Earlier there had only been twelve policemen in the police station: six white and six non-white. But during the morning a series of reinforcements arrived until by lunch time there was a force of nearly 300 armed and uniformed men in addition to five Saracens [tanks]. Yet in spite of the increased force that was then available, no one asked the crowd to disperse and no action was taken to arrange for the defence of the police station. . . .

The Unleashing of Chaos

So the scene was set. Anyone who has lived in the Republic of South Africa knows how explosive that situation had already become. On the one side the ever-growing crowd of noisy Africans—the despised Natives—the Kaffirs who, at all costs, must be kept down lest they step outside the place allotted to them. On the other side the South African police. Every African fears them whether they be traffic police, ordinary constables or members of the dreaded Special Branch. . . .

The only action taken during that morning appears to have come not from the police but from two Pan Africanist leaders who urged the crowd to stay away from the fence around the perimeter of the compound so that they did not damage it. Then [commanding officer of police reinforcements at Sharpeville] Lieutenant Colonel Pienaar arrived in the compound. He appears to have accepted that he had come into a dangerous situation and therefore made no attempt either to use methods of persuasion on the crowd or to attempt to discover what the crowd was waiting for. Instead, about a quarter of an hour after his arrival he gave the order for his men to fall in. A little later he said, "Load five rounds.". . .

During this time Colonel [Att] Spengler, then head of the Special Branch, was arresting two of the leaders of the Pan Africanist Congress. Afterwards he arrested a third man. Colonel Spengler said subsequently that he was able to carry out his arrests because while the crowd was noisy it was not in a violent mood.

It is extremely difficult to know what happened next. Some of the crowd near the gate of the police station compound said later that they heard a shot. Some said that they heard a policeman say, "Fire." Others suddenly became aware that the police were firing in their midst. But all agreed that practically all of them turned and ran away once they realised what was happening. A few, it is true, stood their ground for some seconds, unable to understand that the police were not firing blanks. Lieutenant Colonel Pienaar was quite clear that he did not give the order to fire. Moreover, he declared that he would not have fired in that situation. It was stated later that two white policemen opened fire and that about fifty others followed suit, using service revolvers, rifles and sten guns.

Police Action Causes Devastating Consequences

But whatever doubts there may be of the sequence of events in those fateful minutes, there can be no argument over the devastating consequences of the action of the police on March 21, 1960, in Sharpeville. Sixty-nine people were killed, including eight women and ten children, and of the 180 people who were wounded, thirty-one were women and nineteen were children. According to the evidence of medical practitioners it is clear that the police continued firing after the people began to flee: for, while thirty shots had entered the wounded or killed from the front of their bodies no less than 155 bullets had entered the bodies of the injured and killed from their backs. All this happened in forty seconds, during which time 705 rounds were fired from revolvers and sten guns. . . .

The attitude of the South African Government to the event at Sharpeville can be seen from its reaction to the civil claims

SOUTH AFRICA'S APARTHEID LAWS, 1949–1952

Year	Name	Definition
1950	Prohibition of Mixed Marriages Act	Outlawed marriages between whites and non-whites.
	Immorality Amendment Act	Forbade extra-marital sex between whites and blacks and whites and coloreds.
	Population Registration Act	Required South Africans to be identified and registered from birth as white, colored, Bantu (black), or other.
	Group Areas Act	Set aside separate residential and business areas within cities for different races.
	Suppression of Communism Act	Outlawed communism and the communist party.
1951	Bantu Building Workers Act	Allowed blacks to be trained as artisans in the building trade, but made it a criminal offense for them to do any skilled work in urban areas except those designated for black occupation.
	Separate Representation of Voters Act	Led to the removal of coloreds from the common voters' roll.
	Prevention of Illegal Squatting Act	Empowered the Minister of Native Affairs to force Africans to move off public or privately owned land and authorized local authorities to set up resettlement camps for the squatters.
	Bantu Authorities Act	Set up black homelands and regional authorities and abolished the Native Representative Council.
1952	Natives Laws Amendment Act	Limited the rights of blacks to live in urban areas.
	Natives Abolition of Passes and Coordination of Documents Act (Pass Laws)	Required all nonwhites 16 years or older to carry identification at all times in the form of a pass book or reference book that included their photos, information about their places of origin, employment records, tax payments, and encounters with the police.

Sources: About.com, "African History: Apartheid Legislation in South Africa," www.africanhistory .about.com; The Helen Suzman Foundation, "Key Legislation in the Formation of Apartheid," www.cort land.edu/cgis/suzman/apartheid.html; Padraig O'Malley, "Apartheid Legislation 1948–1990," *O'Malley: The Heart of Hope*, Nelson Mandela Centre of Memory, www.nelsonmandela.org; Wikipedia, "Apartheid Legislation in South Africa," http://en.wikipedia.org.

SOUTH AFRICA'S APARTHEID LAWS, 1953–1970

Year	Name	Definition
1953	Native Labour (Settlement of Disputes) Act	Prohibited strike action by blacks.
	Bantu Education Act	Established a Black Education Department in the Department of Native Affairs tasked with putting together a curriculum that suited the "nature and requirements of the black people."
	Criminal Law Amendment Act	Made illegal passive resistance against any law and introduced whipping as a punishment.
	Reservation of Separate Amenities Act	Forced segregation in all public facilities, buildings, and transport and stated that facilities provided for different races need not be equal.
1954	Natives Resettlement Act	Empowered the government to move blacks from any area within and next to the magisterial district of Johannesburg.
1955	Group Areas Development Act	Set aside in cities separate living areas and business districts for each race.
1956	Natives (Prohibition of Interdicts) Act	Denied blacks the option of appealing to the courts against forced removals.
1957	Immorality Act	Forbade any sexual relations between whites and non-whites.
1959	Extension of University Education Act	Made it a criminal offense for non-white students to register at white universities and provided for the establishment of ethnically based institutions for blacks and separate universities for coloreds and Indians.
	Promotion of Bantu Self-Government Act	Set up distinct 'Bantu Homelands' out of the existing reserves, each with a degree of self-government.
1967	Terrorism Act	Forbade any act of terrorism as well as any recruitment for military training, made participation in terrorist activities a capital crime, and allowed for indefinite detention without trial.
1970	Bantu Homelands Citizens Act	Made all black South Africans citizens of their homelands and took away their South African citizenship.

Sources: About.com, "African History: Apartheid Legislation in South Africa," www.africanhistory .about.com; The Helen Suzman Foundation, "Key Legislation in the Formation of Apartheid," www.cort land.edu/cgis/suzman/apartheid.html; Padraig O'Malley, "Apartheid Legislation 1948–1990," *O'Malley: The Heart of Hope*, Nelson Mandela Centre of Memory, www.nelsonmandela.org; Wikipedia, "Apartheid Legislation in South Africa," http://en.wikipedia.org.

lodged the following September by 224 persons for damages amounting to around £400,000 arising from the Sharpeville killings. The following month the Minister of Justice announced that during the next parliamentary session the Government would introduce legislation to indemnify itself and its officials retrospectively against claims resulting from action taken during the disturbances earlier that year. . . .

Few commentators since Sharpeville have attempted to justify the action of the police that day. In fact, many of them have drawn special attention to the complete failure of the police to attempt to communicate with the crowd at the police station. If it had been a white crowd the police would have tried to find out why they were there and what they wanted. Surely their failure to do so was due to the fact that it never occurred to them, as the custodians of public order, either to negotiate with the African leaders or to try to persuade the crowd to disperse. Their attitude was summed up by the statement of Lieutenant Colonel Pienaar that "the Native mentality does not allow them to gather for a peaceful demonstration. For them to gather means violence.". . .

Opposition to the Pass Laws

It was [the mass of repressive legislation enacted every year since 1948] which was indirectly responsible for the tragedy of Sharpeville, and in particular the "pass laws." Indeed, the immediate cause of many in the crowd assembling at the police station was the growing resentment of Africans to the system of passes. This system originated in 1760 in the Cape Colony to regulate the movement of slaves between the urban and the rural areas. The slaves had to carry passes from their masters. Subsequently, the system was extended in various forms to the whole country and was eventually collated in the Native (Urban Areas) Consolidation Act of 1945. This Act made provision for a variety of passes including registered service contracts and for passes permitting men to seek work in particular areas. But through the years an increasing number of Africans had been given exemption from these laws.

This was the situation which obtained until 1952 when a new act ironically called "The Abolition of Passes Act" made it compulsory for every African male, whether he had previously had to carry passes or no, to carry a reference book. . . . The advent of the reference books meant that technically there were no longer any such things as passes. But . . . to the Africans reference books are passes for they contain all the details which were previously entered on the various pass documents. . . . Even more objectionable than having to possess a reference book is the fact that this book must be produced on demand to any policeman or any of the fifteen different classes of officials who may require to see it. Failure to produce it on demand constitutes an offence for which an African may be detained up to thirty days while inquiries are being made about him. . . .

In 1960 a new development occurred when the Government of South Africa decided for the first time in South African history to extend the pass laws to African women. In their case another fear was added that they might be subjected to manhandling by the police with a further loss of human dignity. In fact, by the time of Sharpeville it was estimated that three-quarters of African women were in possession of reference books. But many of the women who had not obtained reference books were strenuously opposed both to the pass system and to its extension to themselves. To them reference books stood for racial identification, and therefore for racial discrimination. . . .

The Aftermath of the Sharpeville Massacre

Many people inside South Africa, though shocked for a time by the events at Sharpeville, ended by dismissing them as just one incident in the long and growing succession of disturbances that down the years have marked the implementation of apartheid. Certainly the Government of South Africa, though badly shaken in the days immediately following Sharpeville, soon regained control of the situation. On March 24, the Government banned all public meetings in twenty-four magisterial districts. On April 8, the Governor-General signed a proclamation banning the African National Congress and the Pan Africanist Congress as unlawful organisations, the result being that they were both driven underground. But neither of them became dormant. At the same time the Government mobilised the entire Citizen Force, the Permanent Force Reserve, the Citizen Force Reserve and the Reserve of Officers, and the whole of the Commando Force was placed on stand-by. Already on March 30, in Proclamation No. 90, the Governor-General had declared a state of emergency which lasted until August 31, 1960. During that time a large number of prominent opponents of government policy of all races were arrested and detained without being brought to trial. In addition some 20,000 Africans were rounded up, many of whom were released after screening.

So after some months eventually, at least superficially, life in South Africa became at least relatively normal. But underneath the external calm dangerous fires continue to smoulder: fires that can never be extinguished by repressive measures coupled with a constant and growing show of force. Outside South Africa there were widespread reactions to Sharpeville in many countries which in many cases led to positive action against South Africa. . . .

It is my personal belief that history will recognise that Sharpeville marked a watershed in South African affairs. Until Sharpeville, violence for the most part had been used in South Africa by those who were committed to the maintenance of the economic and political domination of the white minority in the Republic. . . .

Until Sharpeville the movements opposed to apartheid were pledged to a policy of non-violence. But on March 21, 1960, when an unarmed African crowd was confronted by 300 heavily armed police supported by five Saracen armoured vehicles, an agonising reappraisal of the situation was inevitable. Small wonder is it that, having tried every peaceful method open to them to secure change without avail, the African leadership decided that violence was the only alternative left to them. Never again would they expose their people to another Sharpeville.

A Student Uprising in Soweto

Denis Herbstein

In the following viewpoint, journalist Denis Herbstein reports on the events that transpired when thousands of black South African high school students marched in the all-black Soweto township in protest of a government edict that the Afrikaans language, as well as English, be used to teach certain subjects. As the number of protestors increased and more police arrived, writes Herbstein, the situation grew worse. After a white officer tear-gassed the crowd and other officers fired into the crowd, students went on a rampage. At least eight people died during the riots that rocked the township. Herbstein, a South African expelled from his homeland in 1976, served as a correspondent for The Guardian, Sunday Times, *and the British Broadcasting Corporation (BBC) and authored several books about South Africa, including* White Man, We Want to Talk to You *and* White Lies: Canon John Collins and the Secret War Against Apartheid.

I n the worst racial clashes since the shootings at Sharpeville [township] 16 years ago [1960], at least eight people died today

[June 16, 1976] during riots in the Johannesburg African township of Soweto.

As a result, black leaders have demanded that the Government should withdraw the ruling that Afrikaans should be taught as a language in Oswego schools. The deaths appear to have followed an incident in which police threw tear gas at high school pupils protesting against the use of Afrikaans.

The eight dead include two white officials of the local Bantu Administration Board, two black adults, three black children and another white man. A further 40 people are in hospital.

The Justice Minister Mr [James Thomas] Kruger said tonight the police "did everything in their power to bring the students under control and were eventually forced to fire warning shots over their heads." From eyewitness reports it is evident that some blacks were killed in this shooting.

Twenty buildings, mostly belonging to the Government, were on fire and many cars were overturned and burnt out. A Johannesburg fire brigade appliance was hijacked by the rioters.

Late tonight police were still having difficulty controlling the situation. Mr Kruger said police were trying to move crowds of people into open areas. The Divisional Inspector of Police in Soweto, Colonel J.J. Gerber, said the police did not "at this stage" think the situation had got so far out of hand that it warranted calling troops, though they had been asked to stand by at two police stations in the township.

Earlier, the police sent their crack anti-urban terrorism unit into Soweto, the first time it has been used. All whites have been evacuated from the township, as well as from the nearby Baragwanath Hospital, the largest in the country.

The Sequence of Events

The riots began when 10,000 high school pupils marched through the huge township (with a population of over 1 million) to demonstrate against the Government's ruling that Afrikaans be used

Rioters in Soweto, South Africa, use burned cars as roadblocks in June 1976. The unrest followed protests against the government decision to teach the Afrikaans language in schools.
© Keystone/Getty Images.

with English as a medium in the teaching of subjects like mathematics, history and geography. Pupils at the Phefeni secondary school in the Orlando West area of Soweto have been on strike since mid-May against the directive.

Striking pupils from other schools joined in, carrying banners with slogans saying "Away with Afrikaans" and "Viva Azania", the name given to South Africa by members of the high school based South African Students' Movement, which figured prominently in the march.

Though the exact sequence of events has not been established, a black newspaper reporter, Miss Sophie Tema, was at the Phefeni School standing behind a group of policemen, mostly blacks, who were facing a taunting crowd of "thousands" of black students. Then about 10 police vehicles arrived, and some 30 policemen got out. The white policemen, she said, were armed with revolvers. The taunting began again.

A white policeman, without warning, then hurled a tear gas canister into the crowd, which immediately began throwing rocks and other missiles at the police. Miss Tema then saw a white policeman pull out his revolver and fire it. Other policemen joined in. They were firing into the crowd, she said. She took a child, aged about seven to a near-by clinic, but he was dead on arrival.

After this students attacked policemen and officials and set fire to buildings and cars over a wide area of Soweto. One white motorist was dragged from his car by students and stabbed to death. The man, an employee of the West Band Administration Board, the Soweto local authority, was still lying at the side of the road some time later. There were also unconfirmed reports that policemen were being held hostage.

The Uprising Has Tragic Results

Another dead white was Dr Maurice Edelstein, chief welfare officer for the Soweto administration. A spokesman for the administration said Mr Edelstein was attacked outside the youth employment centre and later taken to the nearby West Rand hospital by helicopter where officials said he was "dead on arrival."

A seriously injured white who escaped the rampaging mob of schoolchildren on the outskirts of Soweto, Mr Donald J Milella, said afterwards in hospital, "four blacks rescued me from the crowd. As I was pulling away from a stop street in my car, they were all around me. That's the last I remember. The windscreen went, the two side windows went, the back window went and it was just stones coming from all directions."

Mr Milella, who had severe hand and arm injuries, said: "I didn't have a chance to see much. I was too busy protecting myself. I didn't know what was going on. They pulled me out and then four Africans from the shop over the road came to my rescue, pulled me into the shop and put me in the storeroom and told me to stay there and wait for someone to come and fetch me."

South Africa's Bishop Tutu—Time for a Peaceful Solution Is Short

Gary Thatcher

In the following viewpoint, journalist Gary Thatcher spotlights South African cleric and social rights activist Desmond Tutu and his opposition to apartheid policies and practices in South Africa. Tutu's uncompromising position, states Thatcher, has won him a large following among blacks but at the same time has created concern among some whites. Tutu maintains that South African blacks will accept nothing less than full majority rule and warns that a peaceful solution to South Africa's racial problems must be found soon or violence will erupt. Tutu speaks out about white South African acceptance of the treatment of blacks without giving any regard to the morality of that treatment and details reasons why he finds the government's arguments for the creation of "homelands" and its homelands policy totally unacceptable. At the time this viewpoint was written, Thatcher was a correspondent in Africa for The Christian Science Monitor.

There is still time for a peaceful solution to the racial problems of South Africa, says one of this country's harshest government critics. But, he warns, time is rapidly running out.

"There is still an outside chance—just an outside chance—that we may be able to turn the trick [and prevent violence]," says Bishop Desmond Tutu, secretary-general of the South African Council of Churches, "but I say this with a wavering certainly as each day passes."

Bishop Tutu is one of the few remaining black leaders in South Africa who is not banned, held in detention, or convicted and imprisoned for violating one of this country's myriad security laws.

After a brief period outside the country as the Anglican bishop of neighboring Lesotho, this veteran black activist returned to Johannesburg in 1978. Since then, Bishop Tutu has re-emerged as a consistently vociferous critic of the ruling National Party and its policy of "apartheid" (separate development of the races). He appears to have won a substantial black following in the process.

But he spares no criticism of opposition parties as well, arguing that other power-sharing plans—such as "graduated franchise" for blacks—are unacceptable. Only full majority rule, he argues, will satisfy the demands and aspirations of South African black people.

Some Whites Alarmed

This uncompromising stance has alarmed some whites here who regard Bishop Tutu as a threatening figure. In fact, he is a diminutive man, his face framed by gold wire-rimmed spectacles, a gold cross hung around his neck. And contrary to some radical black activists, he insists that nonviolence is still a practical strategy to win political rights for blacks.

His office in the Braamfontein district of Johannesburg is furnished simply. In a manner that is only half-joking, he directs visitors' attention to a small sign on a bookcase alone one wall. It reads: "This room is bugged."

In a low, even voice—punctuated occasionally by quiet sighs—Bishop Tutu chastises the South African Government for intransigence in dealing with black leaders seeking a peaceful resolution of this country's racial conflicts.

"All the black leadership which is still talking about a peaceful solution is beginning to suffer from an erosion of credibility," he says. "Unless we get some significant 'give' we are going to be hard put [to channel black frustrations toward peaceful solutions.]"

Moral Dullness Argued

Many white South Africans, he argues, have too often become dulled to the moral issues surrounding treatment of blacks here. They have accepted arrests, detentions, brutality, and even death of prisoners with little moral outrage, he asserts, because such acts are committed in the name of "enforcing the law."

"Now, something that is 'legal' is ipso facto right. That is one of the most horrible things that has happened in this country."

(According to the South Africa Institute of Race Relations, 128 prisoners died while awaiting trial in 1977, the latest year for which figures are available. This does not include those arrested under various security laws, who are not always afforded a trial.

(Before it was shut down under a government "banning" order, the Christian Institute of South Africa reported that from 1963 to 1977 some 35 such "political" detainees died in government detention.)

Public acceptance of police abuses has led to a general undermining of morality in South Africa, according to Bishop Tutu.

"You can't treat one kind of life as cheap and think that this will not spill over into other areas of life," he says, charging that even South African churches have been derelict by not making an issue of police misconduct.

The bishop admits, however, that immoral acts also have been committed by guerrilla organizations supported by the World Council of Churches (with which the South African Council of Churches is affiliated). The shooting down of civilian airliners by Rhodesian guerrillas, for example, was a "barbarous" act, he says, but he suggests that a sort of moral double standard applies when "the violence structured in this country" doesn't provoke the same worldwide outcry.

His eyebrows alternately rising and wrinkling, Bishop Tutu flatly rejects the government's plan of creating "homelands" in rural areas with the aim of turning them into independent, self-governing black states.

The rejection, he says, is on two grounds: first, that the homelands policy is a unilateral one, adopted by the government without the consent of blacks: second, that the small amount of land set aside for homelands (only 13 percent of the total land area, even though they are theoretically "home" to more than 70 percent of the populace) means these rural reserves cannot be economically viable.

(The South African Government stresses that when only the arable land is included in the total, the homelands claim a larger proportion of the country's "good land." Exact figures are unavailable, however.)

But what if the element of coercion were removed from the homelands policy? That is, what if blacks were not stripped of South African citizenship when their homelands were declared "independent"? Or what if no one was resettled by the South African Government (as some 86,743 people were during a recent 12-month period) into these ethnic reserves?

Bishop Tutu says he still would reject the homelands policy because it reinforces ethnic divisions. "We will not accept the Balkanization of South Africa," he declares.

"Dumping Ground" Seen

So long as the government continues "influx control" measures that limit the number of blacks moving into urban areas, he adds, the homelands will continue to serve as reservoirs of cheap labor, hiding the problem of black poverty and serving as a "dumping ground" for "superfluous appendages" of the South African economy (those too old or poorly trained to work).

Some South African whites—including government officials—argue that blacks are really happier with a simpler, closer-to-nature existence in the homelands. They contend that the homelands protect the tribal life style that is a vital part of the African heritage.

Bishop Tutu bristles at such suggestions, arguing that they are merely pretexts to deny blacks opportunities for economic and political advancement. "Only savages want to go back to nature," he snaps.

Bishop Tutu argues that there is religious justification for the view that blacks will someday govern South Africa.

"Humanly," he concludes, "the situation looks almost hopeless. But we are in this with God. And we are on the winning side, because God is on the side of the oppressed."

The Beginning of the End for Apartheid

F.W. de Klerk

In the following viewpoint, white South African leader F.W. de Klerk informs parliament that negotiation is the key to reconciliation and the only way to ensure enduring peace in South Africa. Reforms must be made. Steps have been taken, de Klerk declares, to rectify injustices in the area of human rights, to institute reform of the death penalty, and to address challenges in the socioeconomic sphere. Immediate steps taken to remove major obstacles in the way of negotiation, he announces, include revoking the ban on major antiapartheid organizations, release from prison of individuals detained purely because of their affiliation with banned organizations, and abolishment of media and education emergency regulations. De Klerk served as president of South Africa from 1989–1994. In 1993 he and Nelson Mandela received the Nobel Peace Prize for their joint efforts to bring about nonracial democracy in South Africa.

M r. Speaker, Members of Parliament.
The general election on September the 6th, 1989, placed our country irrevocably on the road of drastic change. Underlying

F.W. de Klerk, "Address by the State President, Mr. F.W. De Klerk, DMS, at the Opening of the Second Session of the Ninth Parliament of the Republic of South Africa, Cape Town," February 2, 1990. Courtesy of the Government of South Africa.

this is the growing realisation by an increasing number of South Africans that only a negotiated understanding among the representative leaders of the entire population is able to ensure lasting peace.

The alternative is growing violence, tension and conflict. That is unacceptable and in nobody's interest. The well-being of all in this country is linked inextricably to the ability of the leaders to come to terms with one another on a new dispensation. No-one can escape this simple truth.

On its part, the Government will accord the process of negotiation the highest priority. The aim is a totally new and just constitutional dispensation in which every inhabitant will enjoy equal rights, treatment and opportunity in every sphere of endeavour—constitutional, social and economic. . . .

Protecting Human Rights

Some time ago the Government referred the question of the protection of fundamental human rights to the South African Law Commission. This resulted in the Law Commission's interim working document on individual and minority rights. It elicited substantial public interest.

I am satisfied that every individual and organisation in the country has had ample opportunity to make representations to the Law Commission, express criticism freely and make suggestions. At present, the Law Commission is considering the representations received. A final report is expected in the course of this year [1990]. . . .

The Government accepts the principle of the recognition and protection of the fundamental individual rights which form the constitutional basis of most Western democracies. We acknowledge, too, that the most practical way of protecting those rights is vested in a declaration of rights justiciable by an independent judiciary. However, it is clear that a system for the protection of the rights of individuals, minorities and national entities has to form a well-rounded and balanced whole. South Africa has its own national composition and our constitutional dispensation has to take this into account. The formal recognition of individual rights does not mean that the problem of a heterogeneous population will simply disappear. Any new constitution which disregards this reality will be inappropriate and even harmful.

Naturally, the protection of collective, minority and national rights may not bring about an imbalance in respect of individual rights. It is neither the Government's policy nor its intention that any group—in whichever way it may be defined—shall be favoured above or in relation to any of the others.

The Government is requesting the Law Commission to undertake a further task and report on it. This task is directed at the balanced protection in a future constitution of the human rights of all our citizens, as well as of collective units, associations, minorities and nations. This investigation will also serve the purpose of supporting negotiations towards a new constitution.

Reforming the Death Penalty

The death penalty has been the subject of intensive discussion in recent months. However, the Government has been giving its attention to this extremely sensitive issue for some time. On April the 27th, 1989, the honourable Minister of Justice indicated that there was merit in suggestions for reform in this area. Since 1988 in fact, my predecessor and I have been taking decisions on reprieves which have led, in proportion, to a drastic decline in executions.

We have now reached the position in which we are able to make concrete proposals for reform. After the Chief Justice was consulted, and he in turn had consulted the Bench, and after the Government had noted the opinions of academics and other interested parties, the Government decided on the following broad principles from a variety of available options:

- that reform in this area is indicated;
- that the death penalty should be limited as an option

of sentence to extreme cases, and specifically through broadening judicial discretion in the imposition of sentence; and

- that an automatic right of appeal be granted to those under sentence of death. . . .

These proposals require that everybody currently awaiting execution, be accorded the benefit of the proposed new approach. Therefore, all executions have been suspended and no executions will take place until Parliament has taken a final decision on the new proposals. . . .

Revising Socioeconomic Policy

A changed dispensation implies far more than political and constitutional issues. It cannot be pursued successfully in isolation from problems in other spheres of life which demand practical solutions. Poverty, unemployment, housing shortages, inadequate education and training, illiteracy, health needs and numerous other problems still stand in the way of progress and prosperity and an improved quality of life.

The conservation of the physical and human environment is of cardinal importance to the quality of our existence. For this the Government is developing a strategy with the aid of an investigation by the President's Council.

All of these challenges are being dealt with urgently and comprehensively. The capability for this has to be created in an economically accountable manner. Consequently, existing strategies and aims are undergoing a comprehensive revision.

From this will emanate important policy announcements in the socio-economic sphere by the responsible Ministers during the course of the session. One matter about which it is possible to make a concrete announcement, is the Separate Amenities Act, 1953 [to segregate public premises and vehicles]. Pursuant to my speech before the President's Council late last year [1989], I announce that this Act will be repealed during this Session of Parliament. . . .

Nelson Mandela (left) and South African president F.W. de Klerk are awarded the 1993 Nobel Peace Price in Oslo, Norway, three years after South Africa revoked bans on anti-apartheid organizations and released many political prisoners, including Mandela. © AP Images/ John Eeg.

Negotiation Is Key to Reconciliation

Practically every leader agrees that negotiation is the key to reconciliation, peace and a new and just dispensation. However, numerous excuses for refusing to take part, are advanced. Some of the reasons being advanced are valid. Others are merely part of a political chess game. And while the game of chess proceeds, valuable time is being lost.

Against this background I committed the Government during my inauguration to giving active attention to the most important obstacles in the way of negotiation. Today I am able to announce far-reaching decisions in this connection.

I believe that these decisions will shape a new phase in which there will be a movement away from measures which have been seized upon as a justification for confrontation and violence. The emphasis has to move, and will move now, to a debate and discussion of political and economic points of view as part of the process of negotiation. . . .

The steps that have been decided, are the following:

- The prohibition of the African National Congress, the Pan Africanist Congress, the South African Communist Party and a number of subsidiary organisations is being rescinded.
- People serving prison sentences merely because they were members of one of these organisations or because they committed another offence which was merely an offence because a prohibition on one of the organisations was in force, will be identified and released. Prisoners who have been sentenced for other offences such as murder, terrorism or arson are not affected by this.
- The media emergency regulations as well as the education emergency regulations are being abolished in their entirety.
- The security emergency regulations will be amended to still make provision for effective control over visual material pertaining to scenes of unrest.
- The restrictions in terms of the emergency regulations on 33 organisations are being rescinded. . . .
- The conditions imposed in terms of the security emergency regulations on 374 people on their release, are being rescinded and the regulations which provide for such conditions are being abolished.
- The period of detention in terms of the security emergency regulations will be limited henceforth to six months. Detainees also acquire the right to legal representation and a medical practitioner of their own choosing.

These decisions by the Cabinet are in accordance with the Government's declared intention to normalise the political process in South Africa without jeopardising the maintenance of the good order. . . .

Implementation will be immediate and, where necessary, notices will appear in the Government Gazette from tomorrow. . . .

About one matter there should be no doubt. The lifting of the prohibition on the said organisations does not signify in the least the approval or condonation of terrorism or crimes of violence committed under their banner or which may be perpetrated in the future. Equally, it should not be interpreted as a deviation from the Government's principles, among other things, against their economic policy and aspects of their constitutional policy. This will be dealt with in debate and negotiation.

At the same time I wish to emphasise that the maintenance of law and order dare not be jeopardised. The Government will not forsake its duty in this connection. Violence from whichever source, will be fought with all available might. Peaceful protest may not become the springboard for lawlessness, violence and intimidation. . . .

Our country and all its people have been embroiled in conflict, tension and violent struggle for decades. It is time for us to break out of the cycle of violence and break through the peace and reconciliation. The silent majority is yearning for this. The youth deserve it. . . .

Releasing Nelson Mandela
The agenda is open and the overall aims to which we are aspiring should be acceptable to all reasonable South Africans.

Among other things, those aims include a new, democratic constitution; universal franchise; no domination; [equality] before an independent judiciary; the protection of minorities as well as of individual rights; freedom of religion; a sound economy based on proven economic principles and private enterprise; dynamic programmes directed at better education, health services, housing and social conditions for all.

In this connection Mr Nelson Mandela could play an important part. The Government has noted that he has declared himself to be willing to make a constructive contribution to the peaceful political process in South Africa.

I wish to put it plainly that the Government has taken a firm decision to release Mr Mandela [from prison] unconditionally. I am serious about bringing this matter to finality without delay. The Government will take a decision soon on the date of his release. Unfortunately, a further short passage of time is unavoidable. . . .

Today's announcements, in particular, go to the heart of what Black leaders—also Mr Mandela—have been advancing over the years as their reason for having resorted to violence. The allegation has been that the Government did not wish to talk to them and that they were deprived of their right to normal political activity by the prohibition of their organisations.

Without conceding that violence has ever been justified, I wish to say today to those who argued in this manner:

- The Government wishes to talk to all leaders who seek peace.
- The unconditional lifting of the prohibition on the said organisations places everybody in a position to pursue politics freely.
- The justification for violence which was always advanced, no longer exists.

These facts place everybody in South Africa before a fait accompli [an accomplished, irreversible fact]. On the basis of numerous previous statements there is no longer any reasonable excuse for the continuation of violence. The time for talking has arrived and whoever still makes excuses does not really wish to talk. . . .

Henceforth, everybody's political points of view will be tested against their realism, their workability and their fairness. The time for negotiation has arrived. . . .

In my inaugural address I said the following:

All reasonable people in this country—by far the majority—anxiously await a message of hope. It is our responsibility as leaders in all spheres to provide that message realistically, with courage and conviction. If we fail in that, the ensuing chaos, the demise of stability and progress, will forever be held against us.

History has thrust upon the leadership of this country the tremendous responsibility to turn our country away from its present direction of conflict and confrontation. Only we, the leaders of our peoples, can do it.

The eyes of responsible governments across the world are focused on us. The hopes of millions of South Africans are centred around us. The future of Southern Africa depends on us. We dare not falter or fail.

Apartheid Has No Future

Nelson Mandela

On February 11, 1990, antiapartheid activist Nelson Mandela was released from prison after serving twenty-seven years of a life sentence. In the following viewpoint, a speech to the people of Cape Town, South Africa, Mandela thanks both the people worldwide who fought untiringly for his release and those who kept alive the struggle for freedom and democracy for all South Africans. He declares that most South Africans, regardless of color, know that apartheid has no future and explains that the struggle for freedom must be intensified on all fronts to bring about a democratic non-racial and undivided South Africa. The white monopoly on political power has to end, and the political and economic systems must be restructured, states Mandela. Mandela was an internationally recognized antiapartheid leader, Nobel Peace Prize winner, and author. He became president of the African National Congress in 1991 and the first black president of South Africa in 1994.

Amandla! Amandla! i-Afrika, mayibuye! [Power! Power! Africa it is ours!] My friends, comrades and fellow South

Nelson Mandela, "Apartheid Has No Future: Africa Is Ours," *Vital Speeches of the Day*, vol. 56, no. 10, March 1, 1990, pp. 295–297. Reprinted at South African History Online, www.sahistory.org.za. Copyright © n.d. by South African History Online. All rights reserved. Reproduced by permission.

Africans, I greet you all in the name of peace, democracy and freedom for all. I stand here before you not as a prophet but as a humble servant of you, the people.

Your tireless and heroic sacrifices have made it possible for me to be here today. I therefore place the remaining years of my life in your hands.

On this day of my release, I extend my sincere and warmest gratitude to the millions of my compatriots and those in every corner of the globe who have campaigned tirelessly for my release.

I extend special greetings to the people of Cape Town, the city to which, which has been my home for three decades. Your mass marches and other forms of struggle have served as a constant source of strength to all political prisoners.

Mandela Offers Words of Recognition

I salute the African National Congress [ANC]. It has fulfilled our every expectation in its role as leader of the great march to freedom.

I salute our president, Comrade Oliver Tambo, for leading the A.N.C. even under the most difficult circumstances.

I salute the rank-and-file members of the A.N.C. You have sacrificed life and limb in the pursuit of the noble cause of our struggle.

I salute combatants of Umkonto We Sizwe [the military wing of the ANC] . . . who have paid the ultimate price for the freedom of all South Africans.

I salute the South African Communist Party for its steady contribution to the struggle for democracy. You have survived 40 years of unrelenting persecution. . . .

I salute General Secretary Joe Slovo, one of our finest patriots. We are heartened by the fact that the alliance between ourselves and the party remains as strong as it always was.

I salute the United Democratic Front, the National Education Crisis Committee, the South African Youth Congress, the Transvaal and Natal Indian Congresses. And Cosatu [Congress

Nelson Mandela: A South African Icon

Nelson Mandela was born July 18, 1918, in Transkei, South Africa. His father, a chief of the Thembu tribe, expected his son to follow in his footsteps. Instead, he went to the University College of Fort Hare and the University of Witwatersrand and, in 1942, qualified to become a lawyer. Two years later he joined the African National Congress (ANC) and was one of the founders of its Youth League, which sought to spur young people to intensify the fight against segregation in South Africa.

In 1952 Mandela and another ANC member established South Africa's first black law practice. A strong antiapartheid campaigner, in 1956 Mandela was charged with and tried for treason. He had always been a strong advocate of nonviolence, but the 1960 Sharpeville massacre and the government ban on the ANC led him to change his philosophy and propose using violent tactics. In 1961, the same year he was finally acquitted of treason, he helped found Umkhonto we Sizwe, the military wing of the ANC.

In 1962 Mandela was arrested for leading a strike and sentenced to five years in prison. In 1963 he was put on trial with other ANC and Umkhonto we Sizwe leaders for plotting to violently overthrow the government. The following year he was sentenced to life imprisonment. He remained imprisoned, most of the time at Robben Island Prison, until 1990 when, as part of a reform initiative, South African president F.W. de Klerk ordered his release.

In 1991 Mandela was elected president of the ANC. He worked with de Klerk to transition South Africa to a nonracial democracy. In 1993 the two were awarded a Nobel Peace Prize for their efforts. The following year, in an open election, Mandela became South Africa's first black president. In 1995 he established the Truth and Reconciliation Commission and a year later oversaw the making of a new constitution.

Mandela left the presidency in 1999. Although he retired from active politics, he maintained a strong presence worldwide as a promoter of peace, reconciliation, and social justice until his death in 2013.

of SouthAfrican Trade Unions]. And the many other formations of the mass democratic movement.

I also salute the Black Sash and the National Union of South African Students. We note with pride that you have acted as the conscience of white South Africans. Even during the darkest days in the history of our struggle, you held the flag of liberty high. The large-scale mass mobilization of the past few years is one of the key factors which led to the opening of the final chapter of our struggle.

Mandela Tributes Those Who Have Fought Against Apartheid

I extend my greetings to the working class of our country. Your organized stance is the pride of our movement. You remain the most dependable force in the struggle to end exploitation and oppression.

I pay tribute—I pay tribute to the many religious communities who carried the campaign for justice forward when the organizations of our people were silenced.

I greet the traditional leaders of our country. Many among you continue to walk in the footsteps of great heroes. . . .

I pay tribute to the endless heroes of youth. You, the young lions. You the young lions have energized our entire struggle.

I pay tribute to the mothers and wives and sisters of our nation. You are the rock-hard foundation of our struggle. Apartheid has inflicted more pain on you than on anyone else. On this occasion, we thank the world—we thank the world community for their great contribution to the anti-apartheid struggle. Without your support our struggle would not have reached this advanced stage.

The sacrifice of the front-line states will be remembered by South Africans forever.

My salutations will be incomplete without expressing my deep appreciation for the strength given to me during my long and lonely years in prison by my beloved wife and family.

I am convinced that your pain and suffering was far greater than my own.

The Importance of Mass Actions

Before I go any further, I wish to make the point that I intend making only a few preliminary comments at this stage. I will make a more complete statement only after I have had the opportunity to consult with my comrades.

Today the majority of South Africans, black and white, recognize that apartheid has no future. It has to be ended by our own decisive mass actions in order to build peace and security. The mass campaigns of defiance and other actions of our organizations and people can only culminate in the establishment of democracy.

The apartheid destruction on our subcontinent is incalculable. The fabric of family life of millions of my people has been shattered. Millions are homeless and unemployed.

Our economy—our economy lies in ruins and our people are embroiled in political strife. Our resort to the armed struggle in 1960 with the formation of the military wing of A.N.C., Umkonto We Sizwe, was a purely defensive action against the violence of apartheid.

The factors which necessitated the armed struggle still exist today. We have no option but to continue. We express the hope that a climate conducive to a negotiated settlement would be created soon so that there may no longer be the need for the armed struggle.

I am a loyal and disciplined member of the African National Congress. I am, therefore, in full agreement with all of its objectives, strategies and tactics.

The need to unite the people of our country is as important a task now as it always has been. No individual leader is able to take all these enormous tasks on his own. It is our task as leaders to place our views before our organization and to allow the democratic structures to decide on the way forward.

On the question of democratic practice, I feel duty bound to make the point that a leader of the movement is a person who has been democratically elected at a national conference. This is a principle which must be upheld without any exceptions.

Negotiating with the Government

Today, I wish to report to you that my talks with the Government have been aimed at normalizing the political situation in the country. We have not as yet begun discussing the basic demands of the struggle.

I wish to stress that I myself had at no time entered into negotiations about the future of our country, except to insist on a meeting between the A.N.C. and the Government.

Mr. [F.W.] de Klerk has gone further than any other Nationalist president in taking real steps to normalize the situation. However, there are further steps as outlined in the Harare Declaration that have to be met before negotiations on the basic demands of our people can begin.

I reiterate our call for inter alia [among other things] the immediate ending of the state of emergency and the freeing of all, and not only some, political prisoners.

Only such a normalized situation which allows for free political activity can allow us to consult our people in order to obtain a mandate. The people need to be consulted on who will negotiate and on the content of such negotiations.

Negotiations cannot take place—negotiations cannot take up a place above the heads or behind the backs of our people. It is our belief that the future of our country can only be determined by a body which is democratically elected on a nonracial basis.

Negotiations on the dismantling of apartheid will have to address the overwhelming demand of our people for a democratic nonracial and unitary South Africa. There must be an end to white monopoly on political power.

And a fundamental restructuring of our political and economic systems to insure that the inequalities of apartheid are addressed and our society thoroughly democratized.

It must be added that [President] de Klerk himself is a man of integrity who is acutely aware of the dangers of a public figure not honoring his undertakings. But as an organization, we base our policy and strategy on the harsh reality we are faced with, and this reality is that we are still suffering under the policies of the Nationalist Government.

The Need to Intensify the Struggle

Our struggle has reached a decisive moment. We call on our people to seize this moment so that the process toward democracy is rapid and uninterrupted. We have waited too long for our freedom. We can no longer wait. Now is the time to intensify the struggle on all fronts.

To relax our efforts now would be a mistake which generations to come will not be able to forgive. The sight of freedom looming on the horizon should encourage us to redouble our efforts. It is only through disciplined mass action that our victory can be assured.

We call on our white compatriots to join us in the shaping of a new South Africa. The freedom movement is the political home for you, too. We call on the international community to continue the campaign to isolate the apartheid regime.

To lift sanctions now would be to run the risk of aborting the process toward the complete eradication of apartheid. Our march to freedom is irreversible. We must not allow fear to stand in our way.

Universal suffrage on a common voters roll in a united democratic and nonracial South Africa is the only way to peace and racial harmony.

In conclusion, I wish to go to my own words during my trial in 1964. They are as true today as they were then. I wrote: I have fought against white domination, and I have fought against black domination. I have cherished the idea of a democratic and free society in which all persons live together in harmony and with equal opportunities.

It is an ideal which I hope to live for and to achieve. But if needs be, it is an ideal for which I am prepared to die.

My friends, I have no words of eloquence to offer today except to say that the remaining days of my life are in your hands.

I hope you will disperse with discipline. And not a single one of you should do anything which will make other people say that we can't control our own people.

S. Africa Tries Out New System with Risky Plan

Hugh Dellios

In the following viewpoint, journalist Hugh Dellios reports on the ceremony that followed the signing of South Africa's new constitution, the very first in the nation's history to include comprehensive guarantees of human rights for all South Africans. The constitution, explains Dellios, affirms the changeover from white minority rule to a hoped-for multiracial democracy, equality, and human rights. It may prove difficult, he notes, for the nation's leaders to deliver on expectations and reconcile potential constitution-related problems such as those feared by legal experts and those resulting from the Zulu-based Inkatha Freedom Party's reactions to the new document. The article also reports on the pardon given by South Africa's Truth Commission to a former apartheid police commander, an action which, unlike the enactment of the new constitution, may prove extremely controversial. At the time this viewpoint was written, Dellios was a Chicago Tribune *foreign correspondent based in Johannesburg, South Africa.*

Several thousand South Africans returned Tuesday [December 10, 1996] to the scene of one of their country's most notorious crimes of racial oppression and witnessed the simple scribble of a pen that established human rights as the law of the land.

Near the site where 69 protesters were gunned down by police in the 1960 Sharpeville massacre, President Nelson Mandela signed South Africa's new Constitution, sealing a transition from white-minority rule to aspiring multiracial democracy, equality and human rights.

Hours later, South Africa's Truth Commission took another step toward burying the nation's racist past when it announced the first pardon of a former apartheid security officer, a policeman who asked forgiveness for his role in the government-sponsored killings of 11 people in 1988.

A New Beginning with a New Constitution

"Today we cross a critical threshold," Mandela told the crowd at Sharpeville's sports stadium after signing the new constitution.

"Out of the many Sharpevilles which haunt our history was born the unshakeable determination that respect for human life, liberty and well-being must be enshrined as rights beyond the power of any force to diminish. Now, at last, they are embodied in the highest law of our rainbow nation," Mandela said.

The ceremony followed final approval of the constitution last week by the nation's new Constitutional Court. The court had rejected a first draft of the document in September, and lawmakers shored up eight sections dealing with such matters as business-labor relations and provincial powers that the judges had ruled inadequate.

South Africa's new legal blueprint has been hailed for its far-reaching guarantees of human rights. It enshrines a long list of legal protections not spelled out in most constitutions, banning discrimination on the basis of "race, gender, sex, pregnancy, marital status, ethnic or social origin, color, sexual orientation, age, disability, religion, conscience, belief, culture, language and birth."

South African president Nelson Mandela (seated) signs the country's new constitution at a 1996 ceremony in the same sports stadium where the Sharpeville Massacre occurred thirty-six years before. © Charles O'Rear/Corbis.

Facing the Battles Ahead

Now that it is official, South Africa's leaders are under pressure to deliver on expectations. By many accounts that will be difficult. The government already is struggling to deliver adequate housing and education, both also promised in the constitution.

Legal experts also fear the generous constitution could lead to an endless clash of opposing rights in the courts. They foresee legal battles over assisted suicide, pornography, abortion, defamation and protection of the nation's different cultures.

Leon Wessels, deputy chairman of the assembly that wrote the constitution, acknowledged the battles ahead in his speech at Tuesday's ceremony.

"This is only a first step, but it is a definite and determined one," said Wessels, a stalwart of the former ruling National Party. "It was the only way to travel if we wanted to ensure that our rights are transplanted from one generation to another."

Another potential problem for the new constitution is that the Zulu-based Inkatha Freedom Party refused to participate in its drafting. Inkatha officials, upset at reduced authority for provincial and traditional tribal leaders, said they would not feel bound by the new document.

Remembering the Past

The signing ceremony was awash in the emotions of South African history.

The 1960 Sharpeville killings, in which nervous police fired upon marchers protesting "pass laws" that restricted where blacks could go, ignited the most ruthless period of apartheid rule.

Soon after, the government banned the African National Congress and other anti-apartheid groups, and four years later it imprisoned Mandela "for life."

The site of the signing had even deeper importance. Sharpeville is adjacent to the town of Vereeniging, where a peace treaty was signed in 1902 ending the Anglo-Boer War and ushering in a system that denied blacks and "coloreds" the right to vote until the nation's first all-race elections in 1994.

While the constitution's enactment was greeted warmly across South Africa, the Truth Commission's decision Tuesday to pardon former apartheid police commander Brian Mitchell may prove bitterly controversial.

At one point sentenced to death, Mitchell was serving a 30-year prison term for helping plot an assassination of anti-apartheid activists in 1988, a plan that went awry and resulted in the deaths of 11 innocent people in KwaZulu Natal province. In what came to be known as the Trust Feeds massacre, the four police officers assigned to carry out the crime went to the wrong house.

Mitchell is only the fourth person to be granted amnesty out of several thousand who have applied. Commission members ruled that his crime had a political objective, the key requirement for granting a pardon, but some will see the decision as a strategic move to encourage other perpetrators of apartheid crimes to apply for amnesty. The deadline for such applications is Saturday.

Some observers, such as University of Cape Town political scientist David Welsh, said the decision would test the public's tolerance of the commission's efforts to induce truth-telling and reconciliation by offering forgiveness.

"I think people are going to be outraged by this decision," Welsh told Reuters news agency. "Brian Mitchell was convicted of a most horrendous massacre—one that fills everyone with utter revulsion. If they were looking for a sweetener to induce people to come forward, then they couldn't have come up with a better case."

CHAPTER 2

Controversies Surrounding Apartheid in South Africa

Chapter Exercises

SOUTH AFRICAN "HOMELANDS"

ZIMBABWE

BOTSWANA

NAMIBIA

TRANSVAAL

Pretoria

Johannesburg ★

Soweto

SWAZILAND

Upington

Kimberley

ORANGE FREE STATE

Newcastle

NATAL

Alexander Bay

Bloemfontein ★

Pietermaritzburg

Springbok

LESOTHO

Durban

CAPE PROVINCE

ATLANTIC OCEAN

Queenstown

INDIAN OCEAN

Worcester

Cape Town

Port Elizabeth

MOZAMBIQUE

Independent Homelands:
- Bophuthatswana
- Ciskei
- Transkei
- Venda

Self-governing Homelands:
- Gazankulu
- KaNgwane
- Kwa-Ndebele
- Kwazulu
- Lebowa
- Qwaqwa

▲ Nonwhite townships and residential areas

Note: The South African government assigned all Africans to a homeland, or Bantunstan, in an effort to divide ethnic groups into separate nation-states. Members of homelands granted independence became "citizens" of that homeland and had their South African citizenship revoked. No homelands were ever recognized as sovereign states by any other country.

1. Analyze the Map

Question 1: Near which cities are the nonwhite townships and residential areas located?

Question 2: Which self-governing "independent "home-lands lie along South Africa's coast?

Question 3: Which self-governing nonindependent home-lands are in Transvaal?

2. Writing Prompt

Assume you are a South African citizen, and write an editorial expressing your views about whether or not apartheid is the best policy for South Africa.

3. Group Activity

Form groups and debate the following statement: Sanctions are a weapon the international community must use against South Africa's regime in protest of its apartheid policies.

Apartheid Is the Best Policy for South Africa

A.L. Geyer

In the following viewpoint—a speech given to the Rotary Club of London in 1953—South African official A.L. Geyer argues that apartheid is the best solution for all South Africans—black and white alike. South Africa's racial problem, claims Geyer, is different from any other because South Africa is not the original home of black or white Africans; it contains the only independent white nation in Africa; and it is the only independent country in which there are more blacks than whites. Partnership or apartheid, he maintains, are the only alternatives for the future. Partnership is not viable, asserts Geyer, because it would mean national suicide for the whites, while apartheid is a policy of self-preservation, one under which black Africans can develop as a separate people. At the time this speech was given, Geyer was the South African high commissioner in London.

As one of the aftermaths of the last war [the Second Boer War], many people seem to suffer from a neurotic guilt complex with regard to colonies. This has led to a strident denunciation of the Black African's wrongs, real or imaginary, under the white

A.L. Geyer, "The Case for Apartheid, 1953," Union of South Africa Government: Information Pamphlet, August 19, 1953.

man's rule in Africa. It is a denunciation, so shrill and emotional, that the vast debt owed by Black Africa to those same white men is lost sight of (and, incidentally, the Black African is encouraged to forget that debt). Confining myself to that area of which I know at least a very little, Africa south of the Equator, I shall say this without fear of reasonable contradiction: every millimetre of progress in all that vast area is due entirely to the White Man. You are familiar with the cry that came floating over the ocean from the West—a cry that "colonialism" is outmoded and pernicious, a cry that is being vociferously echoed by a certain gentleman in the East. (This refers to Jawaharlal Nehru, Prime Minister of India.)

May I point out that African colonies are of comparatively recent date. Before that time Black Africa did have independence for a thousand years and more—and what did she make of it? One problem, I admit, she did solve most effectively. There was no overpopulation. Interminable savage intertribal wars, witchcraft, disease, famine, and even cannibalism saw to that.

South Africa Is Unique

Let me turn to my subject, to that part of Africa south of the Sahara which, historically, is not part of Black Africa at all—my own country. Its position is unique in Africa as its racial problem is unique in the world.

1. South Africa is no more the original home of its black Africans, the Bantu than it is of its white Africans. Both races went there as colonists and, what is more, as practically contemporary colonists. In some parts the Bantu arrived first, in other parts the Europeans were the first comers.

2. South Africa contains the only independent white nation in all Africa—[a] South African nation which has no other homeland to which it could retreat; a nation which has created a highly developed modern state, and which

occupies a position of inestimable importance.

3. South Africa is the only independent country in the world in which white people are outnumbered by black people. Including all coloured races or peoples the proportion in Brazil is 20 to 1. In South Africa it is 1 to 4.

Why Partnership Is Not a Good Alternative

This brings me to the question of the future. To me there seems to be two possible lines of development: *Apartheid* or Partnership. Partnership means Cooperation of the individual citizens within a single community, irrespective of race. . . . (It) demands that there shall be no discrimination whatsoever in trade and industry, in the professions and the Public Service. Therefore, whether a man is black or a white African, must according to this policy be as irrelevant as whether in London a man is a Scotsman or an Englishman. I take it: that Partnership must also aim at the eventual disappearance of all social segregation based on race. This policy of Partnership admittedly does not envisage immediate adult suffrage. Obviously, however, the loading of the franchise in order to exclude the great majority of the Bantu could be no more than a temporary expedient. . . . (In effect) "there must one day be black domination, in the sense that power must pass to the immense African majority." Need I say more to show that this policy of Partnership could, in South Africa, only mean the eventual disappearance of the white South African nation? And will you be greatly surprised if I tell you that this white nation is not prepared to commit national suicide, not even by slow poisoning? The only alternative is a policy of *apartheid,* the policy of separate development. The germ of this policy is inherent in almost all of our history, implanted there by the force of circumstances. . . . *Apartheid is* a policy of self-preservation. We make no apology for possessing that very natural urge. But it is more than that. It is an attempt at self-preservation in a manner that will enable the Bantu to develop fully as a separate people.

SOUTH AFRICANS' PERCEIVED ADVANTAGES OF APARTHEID, BY INCOME, 1974

Advantages	Upper Income	Upper-Middle Income	Lower-Middle Income	Lower Income	All Respondents
Segregation	12%	10%	10%	12%	10.3%
Wanted by all races	14%	16%	16%	10%	15.4%
Keeps a pure race	2%	13%	14%	12%	13.5%
Social separation of races is good	2%	16%	19%	32%	19.7%
Teaches Bantu self-reliance	10%	2%	5%	5%	4.7%
Prevents inter-marriage	0%	5%	4%	4%	4.3%
Safeguards whites	7%	11%	10%	7%	9.5%
Ensures white supremacy	10%	5%	2%	0%	2.8%
Provides homelands	5%	4%	4%	4%	4.0%
Keeps schools separated	2%	5%	4%	5%	4.3%
Keeps non-whites in their place	0%	1%	3%	3%	2.7%
Keeps towns clean	0%	1%	1%	3%	0.9%
Keeps racial peace	2%	6%	5%	6%	5.0%
Provides Bantu more opportunity	10%	3%	3%	2%	2.5%
Other	0%	2%	1%	2%	1.5%
None	38%	23%	22%	16%	22.0%

Source: Henry Lever, "Opinion Polling in South Africa: Initial Findings," *Public Opinion Quarterly*, vol. 38, no. 3, Autumn 1974, p. 403.

The Immediate Aim Is to Keep the Races Apart

We believe that, for a long time to come, political power will have to remain with the whites, also in the interest of our still very immature Bantu. But we believe also, in the words of a statement by the Dutch Reformed Church in 1950, a Church that favours *apartheid,* that "no people in the world worth their salt, would be content indefinitely with no say or only indirect say in the affairs of the State or in the country's socioeconomic organisation in which decisions are taken about their interests and their future."

The immediate aim is, therefore, to keep the races outside the Bantu areas apart as far as possible, to continue the process of improving the conditions and standards of living of the Bantu, and to give them greater responsibility for their own local affairs. At the same time the long-range aim is to develop the Bantu areas both agriculturally and industrially, with the object of making these areas in every sense the national home of the Bantu—areas in which their interests are paramount, in which to an ever greater degree all professional and other positions are to be occupied by them, and in which they are to receive progressively more and more autonomy.

Apartheid Is an Evil and Unjust System

Desmond Tutu

In the following viewpoint, South African cleric Desmond Tutu speaks out against the South African government policy of apartheid, which he asserts is upheld by a series of harsh and unfair laws. Apartheid, states Tutu, has undermined black family life, given whites a disproportionate share of land, decreed the politics of exclusion, stripped blacks of their South African citizenship and political rights, and given rise to separate and unequal education. It has resulted in unrightful detention, bannings, violence, and death. The cost of apartheid, Tutu proclaims, is too high. Because of apartheid policies, South Africa is a country without justice, peace, or security—a land where widespread unrest will not go away until apartheid is dismantled. At the time this lecture was given in 1984, Tutu was an Anglican bishop, antiapartheid activist, peace campaigner, and Nobel Peace Prize recipient. A year later he became the first black Anglican bishop of Johannesburg.

Before I left South Africa, a land I love passionately, we had an emergency meeting of the Executive Committee of the South African Council of Churches with the leaders of our member

Desmond Tutu, "Nobel Lecture," Nobelprize.org, December 11, 1984. www.nobelprize.org. Adapted by Cengage Learning/Gale. Copyright © 1984 by The Nobel Foundation. All rights reserved. Reproduced by permission.

churches. We called the meeting because of the deepening crisis in our land, which has claimed nearly 200 lives this year alone. We visited some of the trouble-spots on the Witwatersrand [region of northeast South Africa between Vaal River and the city of Johannesburg]. I went with others to the East Rand. We visited the home of an old lady. She told us that she looked after her grandson and the children of neighbors while their parents were at work. One day the police chased some pupils who had been boycotting classes, but they disappeared between the township houses. The police drove down the old lady's street. She was sitting at the back of the house in her kitchen, whilst her charges were playing in the front of the house in the yard. Her daughter rushed into the house, calling out to her to come quickly. The old lady dashed out of the kitchen into the living room. Her grandson had fallen just inside the door, dead. He had been shot in the back by the police. He was 6 years old. A few weeks later, a white mother, trying to register her black servant for work, drove through a black township. Black rioters stoned her car and killed her baby of a few months old, the first white casualty of the current unrest in South Africa. Such deaths are two too many. These are part of the high cost of apartheid.

The Effect of Government Policy on Black Family Life

Every day in a squatter camp near Cape Town, called K.T.C., the authorities have been demolishing flimsy plastic shelters which black mothers have erected because they were taking their marriage vows seriously. They have been reduced to sitting on soaking mattresses, with their household effects strewn round their feet, and whimpering babies on their laps, in the cold Cape winter rain. Every day the authorities have carried out these callous demolitions. What heinous crime have these women committed, to be hounded like criminals in this manner? All they have wanted is to be with their husbands, the fathers of their children. Everywhere else in the world they would be highly commended,

Under apartheid, black men often had no choice but to migrate to white cities for work during most of the year. To keep families together, wives and children would often live in squalid conditions in illegal squatter camps such as this one outside of Cape Town, South Africa, in 1979. © Hulton-Deutsch Collection/Corbis.

but in South Africa, a land which claims to be Christian, and which boasts a public holiday called Family Day, these gallant women are treated so inhumanely, and yet all they want is to have a decent and stable family life. Unfortunately, in the land of their birth, it is a criminal offence for them to live happily with their husbands and the fathers of their children. Black family life is thus being undermined, not accidentally, but by deliberate Government policy. It is part of the price human beings, God's children, are called to pay for apartheid. An unacceptable price.

Inequities of the New Constitution

I come from a beautiful land, richly endowed by God with wonderful natural resources, wide expanses, rolling mountains, singing birds, bright shining stars out of blue skies, with radiant sunshine, golden sunshine. There is enough of the good things that come from God's bounty, there is enough for everyone, but apartheid has confirmed some in their selfishness, causing them to grasp greedily a disproportionate share, the lion's share, because of their power. They have taken 87 [percent] of the land, though being only about 20 [percent] of our population. The rest have had to make do with the remaining 13 [percent]. Apartheid has decreed the politics of exclusion. 73 [percent] of the population is excluded from any meaningful participation in the political decision-making processes of the land of their birth. The new constitution, making provision of three chambers, for whites, coloreds, and Indians, mentions blacks only once, and thereafter ignores them completely. Thus this new constitution, lauded in parts of the West as a step in the right direction, entrenches racism and ethnicity. The constitutional committees are composed in the ratio of 4 whites to 2 coloreds and 1 Indian. 0 black. 2 + 1 can never equal, let alone be more than, 4. Hence this constitution perpetuates by law and entrenches white minority rule. Blacks are expected to exercise their political ambitions in unviable, poverty-stricken, arid, bantustan homelands, ghettoes of misery, inexhaustible reservoirs of cheap black labor, bantustans into which South Africa is being balkanized. Blacks are systematically being stripped of their South African citizenship and being turned into aliens in the land of their birth. . . . The South African Government is smart. Aliens can claim but very few rights, least of all political rights.

Apartheid Dumping Grounds and Discriminatory Education

In pursuance of apartheid's ideological racist dream, over 3,000,000 of God's children have been uprooted from their homes, which have been demolished, whilst they have then been dumped in the bantustan homeland resettlement camps. I say dumped advisedly: only things or rubbish is dumped, not human beings. Apartheid has, however, ensured that God's children, just because they are black, should be treated as if they were things, and not as of infinite value as being created in the image of God. These dumping grounds are far from where work and food can be procured easily. Children starve, suffer from the often irreversible consequences of malnutrition—this happens to them not accidentally, but by deliberate Government policy. They starve in a land that could be the bread basket of Africa, a land that normally is a net exporter of food.

The father leaves his family in the bantustan homeland, there eking out a miserable existence, whilst he, if he is lucky, goes to the so-called white man's town as a migrant, to live an unnatural life in a single sex hostel for 11 months of the year, being prey there to prostitution, drunkenness, and worse. This migratory labor policy is declared Government policy, and has been con-demned, even by the white Dutch Reformed Church, not noted for being quick to criticize the Government, as a cancer in our society. This cancer, eating away at the vitals of black family life, is deliberate Government policy. It is part of the cost of apart-heid, exorbitant in terms of human suffering.

Apartheid has spawned discriminatory education, such as Bantu Education, education for serfdom, ensuring that the Government spends only about one tenth on one black child per annum for education what it spends on a white child. It is educa-tion that is decidedly separate and unequal. It is to be wantonly wasteful of human resources, because so many of God's children are prevented, by deliberate Government policy, from attaining to their fullest potential. South Africa is paying a heavy price already for this iniquitous policy because there is a desperate shortage of skilled manpower, a direct result of the short-sighted schemes of the racist regime. . . .

The High Price of Racial Purity

Apartheid is upheld by a phalanx of iniquitous laws, such as the Population Registration Act, which decrees that all South Africans must be classified ethnically, and duly registered ac-cording to these race categories. Many times, in the same family one child has been classified white whilst another, with a slightly darker hue, has been classified colored, with all the horrible

The 1961 United Nations Resolution on Race Conflict in South Africa

The General Assembly,

Recalling its previous resolutions on the question of race conflict in South Africa resulting from the policies of *apartheid* of the Government of the Union of South Africa, . . .

Recalling also that the Government of the Union of South Africa has failed to comply with the repeated requests and demands of the United Nations and world public opinion and to reconsider or revise its racial policies or to observe its obligations under the Charter,

1. *Deplores* such continued and total disregard by the Government of the Union of South Africa and furthermore its determined aggravation of racial issues by more discriminatory laws and measures and their enforcement, accompanied by violence and bloodshed;

2. *Deprecates* policies based on racial discrimination as reprehensible and repugnant to human dignity;

3. *Requests* all States to consider taking such separate and collective action as is open to them, in conformity with the Charter of the United Nations, to bring about the abandonment of these policies;

4. *Affirms* that the racial policies being pursued by the Government of the Union of South Africa are a flagrant violation of the Charter of the United Nations and the Universal Declaration of Human Rights and are inconsistent with the obligations of a Member State;

5. *Notes with grave concern* that these policies have led to international friction and that their continuance endangers international peace and serenity;

6. *Reminds* the Government of the Union of South Africa of the requirement in Article 2, paragraph 2, of the Charter that all Members shall fulfil in good faith the obligations assumed by them under the Charter;

7. *Calls upon* the Government of the Union of South Africa once again to bring its policies and conduct into conformity with its obligations under the Charter.

United Nations, General Assembly, Official Records, Fifteenth Session, Supplement No. 16A, Resolution No. 1598 *(XV).*

consequences for the latter of being shut out from membership of a greatly privileged caste. There have, as a result, been several child suicides. This is too high a price to pay for racial purity, for it is doubtful whether any end, however desirable, can justify such a means. There are laws, such as the Prohibition of Mixed Marriages Act, which regard marriages between a white and a person of another race as illegal. Race becomes an impediment to a valid marriage. Two persons who have fallen in love are prevented by race from consummating their love in the marriage bond. Something beautiful is made to be sordid and ugly. The Immorality Act decrees that fornication and adultery are illegal if they happen between a white and one of another race. The police are reduced to the level of peeping Toms to catch couples red-handed. Many whites have committed suicide rather than face the disastrous consequences that follow in the train of even just being charged under this law. The cost is too great and intolerable.

Overly Severe Punishment

Such an evil system, totally indefensible by normally acceptable methods, relies on a whole phalanx of draconian laws such as the security legislation which is almost peculiar to South Africa. There are the laws which permit the indefinite detention of persons whom the Minister of Law and Order has decided are a threat to the security of the State. They are detained at his pleasure, in solitary confinement, without access to their family, their own doctor, or a lawyer. That is severe punishment when the evidence apparently available to the Minister has not been tested in an open court. . . . Many, too many, have died mysteriously in detention. All this is too costly in terms of human lives. The minister is able, too, to place people under banning orders without being subjected to the annoyance of the checks and balances of due process. A banned person for 3 or 5 years becomes a non-person, who cannot be quoted during the period of her banning order. She cannot attend a gathering, which means more than one other person. Two persons together talking to a banned person are a gathering! She cannot attend the wedding or funeral of even her own child without special permission. She must be at home from 6:00 PM of one day to 6:00 AM of the next and on all public holidays, and from 6:00 PM on Fridays until 6:00 AM, on Mondays for 3 years. She cannot go on holiday outside the magisterial area to which she has been confined. She cannot go to the cinema, nor to a picnic. That is severe punishment, inflicted without the evidence allegedly justifying it being made available to the banned person, nor having it scrutinized in a court of law. It is a serious erosion and violation of basic human rights, of which blacks have precious few in the land of their birth. They do not enjoy the rights of freedom of movement and association. They do not enjoy freedom of security of tenure, the right to participate in the making of decisions that affect their lives. In short, this land, richly endowed in so many ways, is sadly lacking in justice. . . .

The Government Response to Peaceful Protest

It is against this system that our people have sought to protest peacefully since 1912 at least, with the founding of the African National Congress. They have used the conventional methods of peaceful protest—petitions, demonstrations, deputations, and even a passive resistance campaign. A tribute to our people's commitment to peaceful change is the fact that the only South Africans to win the Nobel Peace Prize are both black. Our people are peace-loving to a fault. The response of the authorities has been an escalating intransigence and violence, the violence of police dogs, tear gas, detention without trial, exile, and even death. Our people protested peacefully against the Pass Laws in 1960, and 69 of them were killed on March 21, 1960, at Sharpeville, many shot in the back running away. Our children protested against inferior education, singing songs and displaying placards and marching peacefully. Many in 1976, on June 16th and subsequent times, were killed or imprisoned.

Over 500 people died in that [Soweto] uprising. Many children went into exile. The whereabouts of many are unknown to their parents. At present, to protest that self-same discriminatory education, and the exclusion of blacks from the new constitutional dispensation, the sham local black government, rising unemployment, increased rents and General Sales Tax, our people have boycotted and demonstrated. They have staged a successful two-day stay away. Over 150 people have been killed. It is far too high a price to pay. . . .

We see before us a land bereft of much justice, and therefore without peace and security. Unrest is endemic, and will remain an unchanging feature of the South African scene until apartheid, the root cause of it all, is finally dismantled. At this time, the Army is being quartered on the civilian population. There is a civil war being waged. South Africans are on either side. When the African National Congress and the Pan-Africanist Congress were banned in 1960, they declared that they had no option but to carry out the armed struggle. . . . The South African situation is violent already, and the primary violence is that of apartheid.

South Africa and Foreign Countries Reacted Differently to the Sharpeville Massacre

Brian Martin

In the following viewpoint, Australian university professor Brian Martin explains that the international reaction to the 1960 Sharpeville massacre was quite different from the one within South Africa. While the international community expressed outrage, the response within South Africa was subdued. He attributes this difference to three factors—less familiarity outside the country with the brutality of apartheid, a lower level of institutionalized racism, and less vulnerability to reprisals from the South African state. From the point of view of most of the world, states Martin, the Sharpeville events involved massive use of force against an unarmed and nonthreatening crowd. Although the South African government and the police took steps to try to minimize the damage to their reputations, their efforts proved futile and, in some instances, counterproductive. Martin is a professor of social sciences at the University of Wollongong in Australia and has authored numerous books and other publications.

On 21 March 1960, white police in the town of Sharpeville, South Africa, opened fire on a large crowd of peaceful black protesters, killing perhaps a hundred of them and injuring many more. This massacre dramatically publicized the protesters' cause internationally. This case starkly illustrates how violent attacks on peaceful protesters can be counter-productive. . . .

The official figure for the number of people killed by the police was 69. [In his book *An Ordinary Atrocity: Sharpeville and Its Massacre*, Philip] Frankel notes that this is certainly too low, as there were 24 or so victims removed by the police, plus others who were injured, removed by family or friends and who later died. It seems reasonable to say perhaps a hundred died. Many more were injured.

Just as important as the number of deaths was the manner by which they occurred. Most of the victims were shot in the back as they fled from the police. The firing continued long enough for some police to reload their weapons and continue. Some police used soft-nosed bullets that cause horrific exit wounds. These antipersonnel bullets, commonly called dumdums, had been banned by the 1899 Hague Declaration; any force that used them would look very bad in world opinion.

Perceptions of South Africa and Apartheid

In 1960, South Africa was a respected member of the international community. It had a long established, well functioning system of representative government, though crucially limited to whites. It had a prosperous economy—again mainly benefiting whites—and was seen as a valuable trading partner. It had many supporters internationally. At the same time, there was considerable opposition to the apartheid system, most obviously among the black South Africans but also among segments of the white population (especially the English-speaking segment) and in many other countries. Among opponents, apartheid was seen as a system of racist oppression.

But only some perceived apartheid as abominable. It had a fairly bland exterior. Apartheid was a system of oppression and exploitation but not one of brutal violence conspicuous to

A street is filled with the dead bodies of Sharpeville Massacre victims in March 21, 1960.
© Keystone-France/Gamma-Keystone via Getty Images.

outsiders. To be sure, the South African police and military were essential to implementation of government policies such as the pass laws, but they mostly appeared as agents of an administrative, routine law-enforcing process, not as outrageous jackbooted thugs.

To many people worldwide, apartheid was abhorrent in itself as a system of racial oppression, irrespective of the legalities by which this was achieved. But in 1960 this view was shared by only a minority of western governments. Colonialism was alive and well. Some countries had gained independence from their colonial rulers, such as India and Pakistan in 1947 and, in Africa, Ghana in 1957, but many others remained colonies, including most of black Africa. In Algeria, nationalists were fighting a bloody war for independence from France. In Vietnam, a liberation struggle was under way against a regime propped up by the U.S. military. Overshadowing the numerous wars around the world was the cold war confrontation between the two superpowers, the Soviet Union and the United States, with nuclear arsenals poised to launch devastating strikes. In the late 1950s, a

powerful peace movement had sprung into existence to oppose atmospheric nuclear testing and the nuclear arms race.

In this context, South Africa seemed a pillar of stability in Africa, where independence movements were agitating for liberation from colonial shackles. The shootings in Sharpeville threatened to undermine international support for South Africa, by providing a stimulus for action by those already opposed to apartheid and by weakening the moral position of the South African government's traditional allies.

An Unjustified Use of Force and Brutality

The shootings, because they were readily interpreted as a brutal attack by white police against the black population, certainly had the potential to be counterproductive for the South African government, for the South African Police as an organizational entity, and for the individual police involved. . . .

From the point of view of most of the world, the Sharpeville events involved massive use of force against an unarmed and non-threatening crowd. The police's heavy use of firearms was seen as totally unjustified. That some in the crowd had sticks and knob-kerries [short clubs with one knobbed end], and that some of them threw stones, did little to challenge the perception that the police had used massive lethal force inappropriately. Albert Luthuli, leader of the ANC [African National Congress], commented that:

> The guns of Sharpeville echoed across the world, and no-where except among totalitarians was there any doubt about the true nature of what had occurred. The Government had placed beyond question the implacable, wanton brutality of their regime. . . .

International and South African Reactions to the Massacre

The international reaction to the massacre was powerful and extensive. [British historian] Peter Calvocoressi, in his book

South Africa and World Opinion, said that, "First emotions were everywhere much the same—horror, indignation, disgust." Governments condemned the massacre. Anti-apartheid activists were galvanized, obtaining much more support than previously. Supporters of the regime were put on the defensive. For example:

> In Norway flags were flown at half-mast on public buildings on the day of the funeral of the Sharpeville victims... the Brazilian government banned a football match in Rio de Janeiro against a South African team; it also recalled its ambassador from Pretoria. At a conference in New Zealand the Prime Minister, Mr. Walter Nash, asked his audience to stand in silent memory of the dead and the Indian House of Representatives also paid this tribute. . . .

By comparison, the reaction inside South Africa was muted. In the face of a government clampdown on activists and all dissent, the black population was demoralized rather than energized by the events. Within Sharpeville itself, apathy was more typical than outrage.

Influencing Factors on the Varied International Response

The difference between international outrage and the subdued response within South Africa can be explained by several factors. Black South Africans were already aware of the iron fist of the apartheid state, through day-to-day encounters with violence and humiliation. For many, the massacre only confirmed what they already knew and so did not cause an explosion of resentment and further action.

Some critics of apartheid saw the massacre as an expression of the true nature of the South African state and immediately assumed the Sharpeville events had been consciously orchestrated by the police as an exercise of premeditated killing for the purposes of intimidation and brutality. . . .

Unlike South African blacks, few international observers were aware of the day-to-day brutality of apartheid, given the carefully managed image of legality and order conveyed by the South African government and the willingness of foreign governments and corporations to ignore evidence that might disturb their political and trading relationships with South Africa. The Sharpeville killings broke through this conventional image, nurtured by ignorance and convenience, with a picture of unmistakable and unconscionable violence. "Sharpeville," a word which became synonymous with the massacre, served as an icon of everything wrong with apartheid.

A second factor distinguishing South African and foreign responses to the massacre was racism. Within white South Africa, blacks were commonly considered inherently inferior. Apartheid was a system of institutionalized oppression— with political, economic, legal, social, and psychological dimensions—that both reflected and enhanced perceptions of white racial superiority and justified privilege. The black population was so devalued that the killings did not generate widespread abhorrence. The victims were perceived as unworthy. Consequently, [according to South African antiapartheid activists Colin and Margaret Legum] South African whites "were staggered by the unanimity of the world's reaction to Sharpeville," reacting with "dazed incomprehension or truculent self-justification."

In contrast, in many foreign countries white racism was neither so virulent nor so widespread. To be sure, white racism was potent internationally, but it had to confront an increasingly powerful worldwide movement for racial equality, which was supported by ringing endorsements from the United Nations and other bodies. The extermination policies of Nazi Germany had discredited white racism in the eyes of many, making it much harder to overtly endorse racist policies, though much overt and de facto racism persisted. Speaking generally, many more people outside South Africa saw the Sharpeville victims as equal members of the human community, in other words as victims worthy of respect and empathy.

A third factor affecting the South African and foreign responses was the potential for intimidation. Within South Africa, police arrested activists as the government strengthened its capacity for repression, declaring a state of emergency. This seems to have discouraged a larger mobilization of resistance. Had the ANC and PAC [Pan Africanist Congress] and other opponents of apartheid been better organized, the massacre might have triggered an expansion of resistance, but, as noted, demoralization was more common. Outside the country, on the other hand, the South African police and state had virtually no capacity for threatening or repressing dissent. The risks of opposing apartheid were far less, making possible a rapid and very public expansion of opposition.

Peer pressure also played a role. Among white South Africans, open support for black equality was not easy. L. F. Beyers Naudé, a South African minister and supporter of white supremacy, began to reconsider his views after the Sharpeville killings. In 1963 he resigned from the ministry "to become a director of a multi-racial Christian Institute." As a result of this challenge to apartheid, he and his family suffered "the fate of every dissenter of prominence in the Church: social ostracism, reinforced by public attack." Ambrose Reeves, Bishop of Johannesburg, who wrote a powerful book about the massacre, was deported from the country.

In summary, there were three factors that helped the massacre trigger a much larger reaction outside South Africa than inside: less familiarity outside the country with the brutality of apartheid; a lower level of institutionalized racism; and less vulnerability to reprisals from the South African state. . . .

The Massacre's Effect on the Government and Police

The Sharpeville massacre was a disaster for the South African government, particularly because it damaged its international reputation. The shooting of protesters, though intimidating to them, had the wider long-term effect of weakening the position of the white police and government in ruling a majority black population. So it is reasonable to say the shooting backfired: it was worse for the government than if it had not happened.

The police and government took a range of steps to reduce outrage from the shooting. . . .

In the end they were mostly unsuccessful: the massacre turned out to be counterproductive for them. Shooting protesters in cold blood was widely perceived as a gross injustice; once information and images about the shooting were communicated internationally, the efforts of the government to blame the protesters and give a semblance of justice through the Wessels Commission [appointed to investigate and report on the Sharpeville massacre] were too little and too late to undo the damage.

Sanctions Should Not Be Imposed on South Africa

Helen Suzman

In the following viewpoint, South African government official Helen Suzman explains why, unlike many black South Africans and members of parliament, she did not believe punitive sanctions should be imposed on South Africa. Implementing sanctions, she states, would cause the economy to shrink and unemployment to increase. It also would lead to chaos in South Africa and impact neighboring states. Sanctions would not help maintain existing jobs or create new ones. Companies that left South Africa would invest somewhere else and most likely not return after apartheid policies had been modified or revoked. There also was a strong likelihood that once overseas companies sold out too cheaply to South African buyers, fewer employer-sponsored social responsibility programs would be offered. Suzman was a white South African legislator and antiapartheid activist who was a member of parliament for thirty-six years.

My opposition to sanctions against South Africa clouded my relationship with many people overseas and with many blacks at home, disappointing those who expected me to be an enthusiastic supporter of punitive action against the regime I opposed over so many years. I believe I had sound economic reasons for my attitude, while as far as the cultural boycott was concerned, it was my belief that contact with the outside world was likely to be more effective than isolation in influencing public opinion in South Africa.

The Effects of Offensive Government Actions

In 1978 I had warned Parliament that the pro-sanctions lobby was gaining ground as a result of the government's offensive actions. Since October 1977, when the government banned eighteen organizations and outlawed [South African newspaper editor and antiapartheid activist] Donald Woods, and [black consciousness leader and antiapartheid activist] Steve Biko's death in detention had hit the headlines, there was a marked stepping up of the campaign, both in the United States and elsewhere, for stronger punitive measures than the 1977 United Nations mandatory arms sanctions. Anti-apartheid organizations in the United States and in Europe which had campaigned for years against investment in South Africa, and which used to be out of court during the annual general meetings of the companies they were targeting, were now finding more receptive audiences. The directors of these companies in many cases threw in the sponge, deciding that the South African connection was just not worth the hassle and threat of boycotts. The *New York Times* said it supported a declaration at the United Nations that South Africa was a threat to peace and expressed the opinion that Export/Import Bank trade credits to South Africa should be ended, and that further investment should be curtailed. It also came out in support of the campus campaign for disinvestment. Indeed, there was a serious crusade developing to force United States companies to divest from South Africa. There was no doubt that this was gaining momentum and support over a very wide field. . . .

Escalation of the Economic Sanctions Campaign

[An] argument used by the government in the sanctions debate was that the hostility aimed at South Africa was engendered by self-interest. I agreed that many countries do have policies dictated by self-interest. But it was also true that South Africa provided one of those rare opportunities in politics where expediency actually coincided with a just cause—the removal of race discrimination. . . .

My warnings, of course, fell on deaf ears, and over the next ten years, to my dismay, every time I went overseas I saw that there was an escalation of the campaign for punitive economic sanctions against South Africa. In 1984 I was in the United States and witnessed the landslide victory of Ronald Reagan and the Republican Party. . . . I felt that the Democrats, in disarray, would be looking around for a rallying point. South Africa and apartheid were an obvious option. I wasn't far wrong. The sanctions lobby in Congress became much more influential. Randall Robinson's TransAfrica organization (a pro-ANC [African National Congress], pro-sanctions lobby in Congress) became more vocal in its demand for punitive measures against South Africa. The hassle factor at the shareholders' meetings on the issue of divestment from South Africa became more pressing. On campuses across the land, the agitation for disinvestment of university pension and trust funds from companies with South African connections became more vehement. State and city governments denied contracts to firms doing business in or with South Africa. Other factors were also operating to reduce economic growth in the country, such as dwindling confidence in South Africa as a good investment risk—which, in June 1986, was the reason for Chase Manhattan Bank's refusal to roll over its loan, rather than moral strictures against apartheid. Although I knew this was earning me hostility at home among former allies and friends and that it engendered bewilderment abroad, I felt it was essential to continue to advance the arguments against economic sanctions. . . .

Reasons Not to Implement Sanctions

Speaking on campuses or to the Council on Foreign Relations or any other organization in the United States, and in writing articles against sanctions for influential publications such as *The New York Times Magazine*, I emphasized that I understood the sincerity of the moral outrage against apartheid and discriminatory practices in South Africa. After all, had I not been fighting them since my first entrance into Parliament back in 1953? But I did not believe that punitive measures which would wreck the economy and reduce the country to chaos would improve the situation. I understood the desire for punitive action; how often had I sat in Parliament and prayed for divine retribution, but, alas, it soon became obvious that if one lived in South Africa, divine retribution was not selective and that the very people one was hoping to help would be adversely affected by the punitive measures. For that reason the implementation of sanctions, which could only cause the economy to shrink and unemployment to increase, was not the answer. The escalating population explosion, about 3 percent a year in the case of black people, meant that jobs had to be provided for about four hundred thousand young black people each year. If these jobs were not provided, South Africa would face an era of increased poverty, violence and crime. Moreover, all the neighboring states around South Africa were more or less dependent on South Africa for job opportunities, for electric power, for the use of ports and transport. Any action taken against South Africa which could adversely affect the economy would inevitably have repercussions in the neighboring states. This was why these countries, although demanding sanctions, continued to trade briskly with us.

It was true that many blacks in South Africa felt that economic sanctions were the only lever to pressure the government into making changes. In addition, some black leaders, such as [South African cleric and activist] Desmond Tutu, averred that "blacks were suffering so much already that a little more suffering caused by unemployment would not make any difference." I disagreed. There is no social security safety net in South Africa, no dole and no food stamps. Unemployment was a dire experience for vast numbers of workers not covered by the unemployment insurance fund. Maintenance of existing jobs and the creation of more jobs was the commitment of every candidate in the United States at election time. Why could this objective be disregarded in the case of South Africa? Survey after survey showed that the answer was "No" when the question "Do you approve of economic sanctions if your own job is in jeopardy?" was posed. The destruction of apartheid was not at issue; that was common cause. The issue was the strategy to be employed.

Certainly there was justification in the challenge by Tutu, that those who were against sanctions must suggest an alternative means of forcing the government to make necessary changes. My view was that it was economic growth which would empower black workers and give their trade unions the muscle to use the only effective weapon at their disposals—industrial action. This differed from economic sanctions because strikes, stayaways and boycotts could be abandoned or reversed when their objective had been obtained, whereas lost markets were not readily regained. When companies disinvested from South Africa, they invested elsewhere and were unlikely to rush back when the political climate had altered. . . .

Furthermore, when overseas companies sold out to South African buyers, generally at fire-sale prices, their social responsibility programs, such as training black employees for managerial positions, extending loans to them for housing, or assisting them in providing scholarships, were often reduced. . . .

The Eminent Persons Group Fails Its Mission

During the 1986 session of Parliament, the visit of the Eminent Persons Group (EPG) took place. It was a seven-person committee of inquiry, sent out by the Commonwealth nations after their summit meeting in the Bahamas in October 1985, and included Malcolm Fraser, former Prime Minister of Australia. The objec-

Workers walk home to the township of New Brighton, South Africa, in April 1985. While much of the international community decided to use sanctions against South Africa as a way of crippling the government, others argued that the resulting unemployment rates would only lead to even more suffering for the black lower class. © William F. Campbell/Time & Life Pictures/Getty Images.

tive was to acquire firsthand knowledge of the South African situation so as to ascertain whether additional sanctions should be imposed if South Africa did not announce its intention to dismantle apartheid, release [antiapartheid activist] Nelson Mandela and other political prisoners, unban the ANC and end the state of emergency. Suspension of violence should be agreed to, to facilitate dialogue and to establish a nonracial representative government. The EPG spent six months in South Africa. . . .

The EPG reported that its mission was a failure. It recommended that consideration be given to further punitive measures, including a ban on air links with South Africa. . . .

In an article in the London *Times*, Fraser argued that the alternative to sanctions was full-scale guerrilla war, from which would emerge a Marxist government that would nationalize everything in sight. . . . Fraser and many people in South Africa and overseas believed, it seemed, that a short, sharp dose of sanctions would cause the fall of the Nationalist government and its replacement by a nonracial democracy. . . .

The Role of Sanctions in the Dismantling of Apartheid

I told my constituents at my 1986 Report Back meeting that what with the EPG, the Commonwealth Summit, the European Community and the U.S. Congress, I had to concede that the battle against sanctions, about which I had frequently warned Parliament with monotonous regularity since 1978, was a lost cause. Notwithstanding the validity of the arguments about the effects on the entire economy of Southern Africa, and despite the somber specter of mass unemployment in South Africa, sanctions were upon us. . . .

The extent to which sanctions were responsible for the dismantling of apartheid is still a contentious issue. Those against sanctions, including myself, concede that sanctions expedited the process, but also are of the opinion that the claim of the pro-sanctions lobby—that the imposition of punitive measures was the major reason for [South African president F.W.] de Klerk's about-turn—ignores many factors.

One of them was the demise of communism in the USSR [Soviet Union] and Eastern Europe, which deprived the National Party government of its contention that it was the main bulwark against communism on the African continent. Thus the justification for arbitrary measures as a defense against the "total onslaught" of communism could no longer be used.

Another was that many major changes took place before the American Congress passed the Anti-Apartheid Act, with its widely ranging trade and other strictures, in November 1986, and before the European Community increased its sanctions against South Africa.

Finally, the escalating resistance of black, Colored and Indian people is not given the prominence it deserves in undermining the apartheid system.

But the argument about the efficacy of sanctions, disinvestment and divestment is now irrelevant to the task at hand. A high price was paid in economic terms by the thousands of people who lost their jobs in the labor-intensive sectors of the economy such as agriculture and coal mining, and in an area like Port Elizabeth, in the Eastern Cape, where economic devastation followed divestment by the American motor car companies. Recovery of the economy, the creation of jobs and the provision of housing and education must now be the priority considerations. And those countries, organizations and individuals that advocated punitive measures surely now have a major responsibility to encourage investment, to stimulate economic activity and to exert their influence to rescue South Africa from the poverty and violence engulfing the country. Inheriting a wasteland will not benefit any of the groups presently vying for power.

US Companies May Not Truly Be Leaving South Africa

Charles Villa-Vicencio

In the following viewpoint, South African–born professor Charles Villa-Vicencio contends that the argument some US companies have used against withdrawal from South Africa is neither sincere nor valid. Even the companies that have announced they are leaving South Africa and are selling off their South African subsidiaries are not completely withdrawing from the country, argues Villa-Vicencio—they are merely changing the way in which they are involved. At the time this viewpoint was written, Villa-Vicencio was a professor of religious studies at the University of Cape Town. He later served as national research director for the South African Truth and Reconciliation Commission, after which he founded the Institute for Justice and Reconciliation in Cape Town.

The argument for and against the withdrawal of U.S. companies from South Africa continues, despite sanctions legislation and the recent sale of several U.S. subsidiaries in this country. The essence of the argument against withdrawal is that "blacks will suffer most" and that with the exception of a few radicals, the majority of black workers are against both disinvestment and sanctions.

Workers enter the building of a US-based company in South Africa in 1985. At the time, the United States was beginning antiapartheid efforts, including sanctions and other restrictions. © Selwyn Tait/Time & Life Pictures/Getty Images.

Polls among urban blacks, invariably conducted by liberal academics in South Africa and quoted ad nauseam by spokesmen for U.S. firms, are purported to "verify" this. Armed with these surveys, multinationals have vowed to stay put for the sake of black workers and the promotion of black management.

It is difficult not to be suspicious of the motives of managements that suddenly begin to advocate the cause of their deprived workers. And suspicion turns to cynicism when these altruistic firms, such as Coca-Cola Co., General Electric, General Motors Corp., International Business Machines Corp. and Honeywell Inc. begin to withdraw.

Disinvestment Has Community Support

South African sociologist Mark Orkin, in his 1986 book, *Disinvestment, the Struggle and the Future*, reveals the simplistic and ideological bias of the opinion surveys and suggests that 73% of urban black workers favor total or conditional disinvestment.

US Disinvestment from South Africa

The move by transnational corporations out of South Africa began in 1984 when at least 10 United States corporations withdrew their operations from the country. . . . From the beginning of 1984 until July 1988, a total of 339 identifiable corporations from 15 countries reduced or terminated their exposure to South Africa. . . . These withdrawals ranged in form from the closure of a sales or representative office to the sale of a subsidiary as an ongoing operation and to the complete shutdown of a fully operational subsidiary. . . .

The prevalence of disinvestment among United States firms can be attributed to a number of factors, foremost among which is the strength of corporate campaigns in the United States. Antiapartheid activists have very effectively targeted companies through shareholder resolutions, portfolio divestment policies, consumer boycotts and, most importantly, selective purchasing legislation. A number of companies have cited the latter strategy, which has an immediate and recognizable impact on a company's domestic sales, as the reason for their decision to pull out of South Africa. The United States also enjoys a much wider acceptability of the notion of corporate accountability and disclosure than do most other countries. United States corporations in South Africa may also act with greater independence than European firms that participate more frequently in joint ventures with local firms and therefore have a stronger South African identity.

Beate Klein, "Transnational Corporate Disinvestment from Africa: Selective Disengagement" in United Nations Centre Against Apartheid: Notes and Documents, *vol. 13, no. 88, August 1988, pp. 6–7.*

Archbishop Desmond M. Tutu insists that neither he nor any other black leader specifically wants sanctions. They believe, however, that it is one of the few options left. "There is no guarantee that sanctions will topple apartheid," Tutu said, "but it is the last nonviolent option left." This perception clearly has broad-based community support, with an increasing number of trade unions, churches and other groups supporting some form of disinvestment.

But what is the projected effect of these withdrawals? IBM has announced that it will continue its social-responsibility programs, contending in a full-page newspaper ad that its South African operation has been sold to a new company "for the benefit of employees of IBM South Africa." GM, in turn, assures its customers that the future South African-operated company will be "run in a manner suited to South African markets."

Have U.S. companies suddenly developed social consciences? Who is to benefit from the proposed withdrawals? Has the anti-apartheid lobby convinced these companies that the hassle factor is no longer worth it? More important, are these withdrawals for real?

Companies Are Not Truly Withdrawing from South Africa

American companies for some time now have been operating under the restraints of the Sullivan Principles and U.S. legislation prohibiting the sale of products to the South African government police and military. IBM chairman John Akers is quoted as saying the local subsidiary is being sold "before our freedom of action is further limited." GM reports that it has not made a profit in South Africa since 1981.

In this situation it makes sense for these companies to sell off their South African subsidiaries. With fewer restrictions facing local companies and the increasing possibility of a lucrative market (albeit a covert one) in the government and military sector, U.S. companies will be able to concentrate on collecting royalties and profits from the sale of technology and equipment. Thus by "pulling out" of South Africa, these U.S. companies can increase their profits and avoid the anti-apartheid hassles. Rather than withdrawing in any real sense, these companies simply are changing their form of involvement.

Rumors abound concerning the bargain-basement prices paid to IBM, GM and others for their subsidiaries by local firms, with the short-term effect benefiting the coffers of South African white entrepreneurs, while black employees are left dependent on their good will. All political strategies have a payoff and blacks seem to be saying this is a price they are prepared to pay or, as is often stated, "at least we will be suffering with a specific goal in mind."

The Potential Effects of Disinvestment

But what is the loss factor for South Africa? The sale of U.S.-owned companies means an important loss of foreign exchange; Western vested interest in the country is diminished. The sanctions-disinvestment package also is an important part of a strategy to isolate this country.

The kind of U.S. withdrawal presently being practiced could further elicit an intensification of the sanctions lobby if there is any hint of these newly acquired South African companies supplying equipment and technology of U.S. origin to either the government or the military. Should sanctions be extended to preclude all these possibilities, they would come close to being total.

Because South Africa is so dependent on computer technology from the United States and other countries, total sanctions would have a devastating effect—not only on the economy but also on the technological well-being of the country. So while the immediate effect of the U.S. companies' actions on the South African economy is not extensive, it does represent a further turn of a screw that is likely to be tightened a lot more before this country submits to the inevitable.

Multiple Factors Caused the Collapse of Apartheid

Kathleen C. Schwartzman and Kristie A. Taylor

In the following viewpoint, University of Arizona colleagues Kathleen C. Schwartzman and Kristie A. Taylor analyze the declining support among whites for South Africa's apartheid regime and the effect it had on the government and the system. The authors conclude that several factors brought an end to apartheid in South Africa: both South African capitalists and foreign capital investors played a part, as did South African protesters and concerned individuals, groups, and organizations in other countries who refused to buy South African products. The authors doubt that the joint actions of the protestors and the international boycotters alone could have harmed the government enough to bring about change; their actions had to coincide with the opposition by the South African capitalists and foreign capital investors. Schwartzman is an associate professor at the University of Arizona. At the time this viewpoint was written, Taylor was a graduate student at the University of Arizona.

Numerous theories offer explanations for the recent transitions to democratic rule [in South Africa]. Some argue that

Kathleen C. Schwartzman and Kristie A. Taylor, "What Caused the Collapse of Apartheid?," *Journal of Political and Military Sociology*, vol. 27, no. 1, 1999.

the transitions to democracy were the result of social protest. Others attribute democratization to the rise of an industrial labor force and workers' struggles. Some highlight external factors that produced democratic transitions, either by direct imposition of democracy or by an indirect effect of economic sanctions against a nondemocratic regime. Many South African observers, on the other hand, have argued that labor-market distortions would produce economic stagnation which would, in turn, force a transition.

The first fully democratic election in South Africa was held in 1994, only four years after [F.W.] de Klerk assumed the presidency and freed [antiapartheid activist] Nelson Mandela and only two years after the [national] referendum. The transition to a full democracy certainly moved at high speed. Such rapid change suggests a preexisting willingness to accept the transition, a willingness that may have reflected the declining legitimacy of the apartheid regime. While the apartheid regime systematically lacked legitimacy among the black population, its legitimacy ebbed and flowed for the white population. Because the final collapse of apartheid resulted from a negotiated transition rather than a violent overthrow, we have focused primarily on the declining support among whites. . . .

The Decline of White Support for Apartheid

Opinion polls taken in South Africa revealed general pessimism. In 1981, 47% of the white population thought that unemployment would increase in the next year. In 1984, over 52% thought that the world would be a worse place for them to live in 10 years. In 1990, only 21% of the white population thought that they were better off compared with the past, whereas 46% thought they were worse off. A voter commented in a 1992 exit poll, "We have to think of our economy, sport and the rest of it. I can't see any other way. We must go forward now." A poll published by the *Johannesburg Star* reported that 80% of an all-race sample opposed sanctions and 75% opposed disinvestment. What accounts for the decline in the feeling of well-being? What accounts for people's willingness to pull the plug on apartheid? The malaise appears to have accompanied the decline in per-capita income, and for many, that was a direct result of government actions. . . .

Despite significant global noncompliance, the South African elite did suffer from anti-apartheid protests and economic sanctions. As a result, leaders first attempted economic reforms without altering the essence of apartheid. The 1985 refusal by foreign banks to roll over South Africa's loans was followed by modifications in the facade of apartheid, for example, the pass laws were scrapped and property rights were granted to blacks. Sanctions, however, forced Pretoria to pay a price for apartheid, persuading some of the need for more substantial reforms. . . .

In 1988, three years after the 1985 debt crisis, South Africa registered its first balance-of-payments deficit. Bankers reluctantly called for more austere economic policies. While such policies would help the deficit by discouraging imports, they would also risk alienating voters before upcoming municipal elections. Leaders expressed concern about the effect of an economic crisis on the legitimacy of the government. The sanctions and corporate disinvestment split the white community, sparked disagreements among businessmen and economists, and divided the black community. Economic solvency had been inextricably bound to apartheid and its caretaker government. The remedy was clear. As Mr. De Lick, head of the South African Reserve Bank put it, "Economic recovery required political changes that would appease overseas critics sufficiently for capital to start flowing back." The crisis required a political solution.

This dissension within the capitalist class upset the ruling coalition: "Cracks began to appear in the white power bloc as business leaders despaired of seeing reforms implemented and repression failed, and [all the] while the white working class was losing its privileged position in the National party." . . .

Historically, South Africa's growth had been fueled by the apartheid labor system: "The discovery of diamonds in 1867 and gold in 1886 constituted the beginning of a century of growth . . . that was among the fastest in the world." Until at least World War II, mining growth (particularly in gold) was built upon an unlimited supply of cheap unskilled labor. The need for skilled labor rose after World War II when the manufacturing sector displaced mining in contributions to the GDP [gross domestic product]. Skilled labor, however, remained the monopoly of white workers. This meant that eventually the manufacturing sector faced an inadequate supply of skilled labor and increased labor costs. Shortages of skilled labor were an unintended consequence of the apartheid system, where racial principles supplanted market ones. In the past, two solutions—importing workers and whittling away at the color bar—had been used. Each was exhausted, and employers expressed concern about the insufficiency of artisans and apprentices to service modern industry.

For some time, skilled labor shortages had been offset by training unskilled whites migrating from rural areas, and by encouraging white emigration from other countries. . . .

Economic Pressure on the Apartheid System

However, the [1976] Soweto uprising and the new requirement that foreign nationals participate in the military slowed these migratory flows. By 1986, South Africa had recorded its largest net migration loss since World War II.

A potential solution to the skilled-labor shortage problem rested with nonwhites. Business leaders believed that the only way to obtain the necessary stable, skilled workforce to staff a technologically sophisticated mining and manufacturing industry was to upgrade the townships, invest in education, and give a modicum of political rights. In the interim, employers designed anti-apartheid innovations that would allow Africans to do the work technically reserved for whites. One such innovation was to subdivide a given task formerly carried out by whites, leaving a skilled and better-paying part for whites and a less-skilled and lower paying part for blacks: "Even the armed forces . . . had to begin recruiting non-whites in the early 1970." Nevertheless, such encroachments across the apartheid labor line were insufficient to redress the labor shortages, and the business community expressed a desire for race-free employment practices.

By 1990, apartheid was an anachronism that prevented the economy from maintaining its former growth rate. . . . The apartheid-generated skilled-labor bottleneck was exacerbated by two trends: the development of more technologically advanced industries (capital goods sector) and the movement of skilled whites out of manufacturing into the service sector. The reality of contemporary South Africa was that apartheid-driven decisions contradicted labor-market decisions. . . .

Two other unintended consequences of the apartheid labor system are identifiable: 1) the diminished purchasing power of the masses and 2) a more costly white labor force. . . . The white consumer community, because of its small size, was incapable of driving economic growth. Second, the color bar system, which was intended to prevent black Africans from holding jobs intended for whites, created a more expensive labor force that could not be cheapened through an increase in the labor supply.

Many agree that by the mid-1970s South Africa had begun to suffer from "the structural constraints posed by apartheid, with its requirements of duplicate administrations, additional military and police expenditures, restrictions on the growth of domestic markets and skilled labor among blacks, and inefficient investment to offset the oil and arms embargoes."

The Effect of Foreign Economic Sanctions

Members of the international community maintained that South African rulers would only end apartheid when they saw no other alternative. Trade and investment embargoes were the weapon of choice against racial discrimination. Without embargoes, it was thought, South Africa would pursue a reformist option—

conceding to the black community some socioeconomic gains but no political rights.

Evaluations of the impact of international embargoes range from a positive assessment . . . to a negative . . . and created a backlash among the white electorate, who turned toward ultra-right-wing parties in the 1987 general election. . . .

The arms embargo prevented South Africa from modernizing its air force and weakened its navy almost to the point of collapse. At the same time, the unintended consequence of the arms boycott was the promotion of a state arms import-substitution industry (Armscor) which not only was able to fill part of the arms gap, but by 1986 was a driving force in the economy. . . .

The South African economy was dependent upon foreign capital inflows to finance the excess of investment over savings and to balance its current account. South Africa was a net importer of capital, in part owing to the capital hungry nature of mining. Conditions also had been favorable for investors: "A policy of import substitution, attractive profits from mineral resources, low wages and high profitability during the apartheid boom period encouraged high levels of direct foreign investment." While we cannot sort out their relative weights, the international sanctions campaign and domestic political instability both discouraged foreign capital flows. . . .

International sanctions affected foreign capital inflow. The actions of international anti-apartheid groups expanded in the 1980s, and by 1986 over twenty state governments and some institutional investors had been persuaded to divest their pension funds of stocks from companies operating in South Africa. . . . It is unlikely that the sanctions would have escalated had it not been for the domestic protest. . . . In 1977, the year following the Soweto uprising, not only was there a large outflow of capital but also no new loans were forthcoming, leading to an overall decline in investment. The turmoil of the 1980s brought net capital inflows to an end. The foreign investment climate had turned sour. In its 1982 edition, the publication *Business Environment*

Risk Information advised businessmen against long term involvement in South Africa ranking it a "prohibitive" risk." . . . By the end of 1987, some 40% of foreign subsidiaries operating in South Africa had disinvested.". . . Domestic sources were unable to compensate for the loss. . . .

The Role of the International Banks

Many observers think that multinational banks inflicted the greatest damage on the South African economy in July 1985, when they called in the loans. After 1984, a year that was punctuated with massive protests and upheavals in townships and factories, South Africa's risk factor also became apparent to international bankers. . . . The growing political instability brought panic to the international financial community, which could no longer "discount" the enormous short-term debt. . . . Restricted access to international investment and lending was an important source of pressure for change.

The international sanctions movement had hitched foreign capital flows to apartheid. Neither the state's fiscal crisis nor the general economic crisis could be solved without a modification of the apartheid system. By 1986, associations representing three-fourths of the business community were asking for reforms in the apartheid system, such as an end to the pass laws and forced relocation. The governor of the Reserve Bank lamented in 1987 that the lack of apartheid reforms affected business and consumer confidence. The president of the Chamber of Mines said, "I feel strongly that the counter to U.S. disinvestment threats lies in South Africa's internal constitutional and general reform process." These accounts of sanctions offer support for our hypothesis that external factors provoked the collapse of apartheid or, more specifically, that the loss of export earnings and of foreign investment and loans dampened growth to the extent that white South Africans (citizens and members of the business community) were forced to concede the unworkability of apartheid. . . .

The Effects of Domestic Social Protest

During the four-and-a-half decades of apartheid, black South Africans—who bore the full weight of apartheid—waged a continuous battle against that regime. Opposition was organized by a number of groups such as the African National Congress (ANC), the South African Communist party, and the United Democratic Front (UDF)—an alliance of more than 600 organized anti-apartheid protest groups. The ANC trained thousands of exiles to carry out sabotage missions and incite unrest aimed at rendering the townships ungovernable. Some of the better publicized protests include: Sharpeville in 1960, the Soweto uprising in 1976 (in which authorities killed an estimated 1,000 people), student boycotts in 1984, and a rent strike in Soweto in 1986. These boycotts, stayaways and violent protests peaked in 1986 and led to the imposition of a state of emergency.

The opposition death count was high. At least 2,500 black South Africans were killed in political violence between September 1984 and December 1986. And between 1987 and 1991, 5,000 blacks died in bloody clashes with police, army, or rival black groups such as the government-sponsored Inkatha party. [Political scientist] Anthony Marx concludes that the impact of social movements on the democratic transition was greatest after 1979, when the emphasis of the opposition movement shifted from ideological realignment and unity to action. Rather than the unorganized outbursts of the early years, after 1987 more than one-third of Soweto residents belonged to a union or community organization. General strikes in local areas demonstrated the level of organization achieved in townships combining community, student, and union groups.

The government responded with repression. In 1976 the government banned outdoor political meetings; in 1984 and 1985, the government, in response to nationwide uprisings, sent troops into the townships and declared a state of emergency. In July of 1985, the banning of outdoor political meetings in townships was extended to funerals for victims of civil unrest.

A street in front of white-owned stores is empty during a 1985 boycott by blacks in protest of apartheid. © William F. Campbell/Time Life Pictures/Getty Images.

As a result of this unrest, the average daily prison population in December 1985 rose to 113,792. . . . Still, the government's prisons, prohibitions, and states of emergency were unable to silence the opposition.

Civil unrest contributed to the state's fiscal difficulties. The maintenance and defense of apartheid created voracious bureaucratic and military apparatuses. Such state expenditures jeopardized the funding on black education which had been undertaken to address the needs of business and industry. . . .

Rising apartheid-driven expenditures forced the government to reduce the share of national income that went to white civil servants—the main beneficiaries of apartheid—and to reduce the amount of government investment in national savings. The fiscal crisis led President [P.W.] Botha, as early as 1988, to introduce a much reduced government budget, including wage freezes for public-sector employees and a privatization of some parastatal [quasi-governmental] firms. The high costs of apartheid converted South Africa into a high-tax country. . . . In conclusion, protest activity exacerbated the fiscal crisis, which in turn created discontent among apartheid's supporters. . . .

Factors That Dismantled Apartheid

The history of the South African political regime in the post–World War II period can be described using [a] model of the interwar regimes in Southern Europe. Obviously, the South African regime differs from Europe in that apartheid was principally a racial state. . . . Like Italy and Portugal, South Africa had a state that not only suppressed liberal democracy and class conflict but also constrained the market economy. Apartheid labor legislation may have initially contributed to capital accumulation, but it also restricted labor mobility across economic sectors and across space. What this literature suggests is that economic changes and ensuing labor-force changes posed a challenge to the political system.

The South African industrial sector grew significantly between 1930 and 1960. After 1960, manufacturing expanded at a faster rate than the overall economy. Manufacturing employment doubled between 1960 and 1975. Some of the new employment came from the auto industry, which, after 1961, was promoted through a series of domestic content laws. These new industrial concentrations opened up new possibilities for working class conflict. Strikes, which started in Durban and spread throughout the country, reflected a growing dissatisfaction with wages, rising prices, and lack of housing. Such unrest resulted in the 1973 legislation which legalized strike. . . . The oil crisis of 1973 led the South African government to promote the production of capital goods. This phase of industrialization gave birth to a new capital-goods working class and a new unionism. . . . In the 1980s, strikes, stayaways, boycotts, factory occupations, and other forms of protest spread throughout the country. . . .

We hypothesize that . . . the rising labor struggles which accompanied the new industrial order contributed to the willingness to abandon apartheid. . . .

Who brought an end to apartheid? Our findings suggest that those factors responsible for the collapse of apartheid include (in order of importance): 1) domestic capitalists, whose growth was restricted by the artificially high-priced labor, 2) foreign capital investors, who saw disincentives to investing, and 3) domestic protesters and sympathetic international boycotters of South African products who took joint actions. If the opposition to apartheid was confined to domestic protest, apartheid might have endured even longer. Bloody and violent protesting had gone on, after all, for decades. It is also questionable whether the joint actions of protesters and international product boycotters could have done sufficient damage to the legitimacy of the apartheid regime were they not coterminous with the opposition of the first two.

The Truth and Reconciliation Commission Was Successful

Njabulo S. Ndebele

In the following viewpoint, academic and writer Njabulo S. Ndebele explains why compromise was needed in South Africa and how the Truth and Reconciliation Commission (TRC) hearings helped in the reconciliation process. The TRC, contends Ndebele, was successful; it made South Africans face up to the nation's history of racism, especially over the previous fifty years, and make needed social arrangements. It contributed greatly to reconciliation by addressing the human rights violations of both the apartheid government and the liberation movements, asserts Ndebele. That there is little or no likelihood that the South African state will crumble in the near future due to racial conflict is an important measure of the TRC's success, he concludes. Ndebele is currently chancellor of the University of Johannesburg.

In his book *Tomorrow is Another Country*, South African journalist Allister Sparks describes how Nelson Mandela's African National Congress (ANC), and the apartheid government of South Africa were forced to recognize the need for a negotiated settlement. In a crucial meeting between the ANC and the

Njabulo S. Ndebele, "South Africa: Quandaries of Compromise," *UNESCO Courier*, December 1999, pp. 22–23. Copyright © 1999 by UNESCO. Used with permission. All rights reserved.

right-wing generals of the South African armed forces, Mandela declared:

> "If you want to go to war, I must be honest and admit that we cannot stand up to you on the battlefield. We don't have the resources. It will be a long and bitter struggle, many people will die and the country may be reduced to ashes. But you must remember two things. You cannot win because of our numbers: you cannot kill us all. And you cannot win because of the international community. They will rally to our support and they will stand with us." [South African military commander] General [Constand] Viljoen was forced to agree. The two men looked at each other . . . [and] faced the truth of their mutual dependency.

This declaration, and its acceptance by everyone at that meeting, illustrates one of the major factors that led to the foundation of the Truth and Reconciliation Commission (TRC) in 1995. The basis of any compromise is that contending parties display a willingness to give up irreconcilable goals, and then enter into an agreement that yields substantial benefits to all parties. The apartheid government of South Africa desired to continue to hold on to the reins of power, but was willing to allow for increased political participation by blacks. The liberation movement, on the other hand, desired the complete removal of white power. Neither of these goals seemed achievable without an all-out war. It seemed in the best interest of all to avoid such a situation.

Creating a Conditional Amnesty Process

One of the demands of the beleaguered apartheid government was that in exchange for loss of power there should be a blanket amnesty for all the agents of apartheid, particularly the police and the armed forces. But while such an outcome would be beneficial to whites, it would not enjoy the support of those who were victims of apartheid. They would rightly feel that the beneficiaries and enforcers of apartheid were getting away too easily.

The Truth and Reconciliation Commission Helped South Africa Transition to a Full Democracy

Dullah Omar, the Minister of Justice in Nelson Mandela's first government, introduced in 1995 legislation into the first democratic Parliament to establish a Commission to deal with "the conflicts of the past." The Commission would not only to find out what had happened in the past, but would grant amnesty from prosecution to those who made full disclosure of what had happened. The Promotion of National Unity and Reconciliation Act was approved by parliament after much debate in July 1995. . . .

It was decided that the hearings should be in public unless there was a very strong reason not to. . . . The Commission was designed to bring about a process of healing, and for that a public catharsis was needed. After the hearings, it was hoped, the country could "put the past behind it" and move into a new future, after the truth about the conflicts of the past had been revealed and a measure of reconciliation achieved.

The worst outcome of such a solution would be that black South Africans, victims of apartheid, would lose confidence in any of their leaders who could accept such a solution.

The flaw in this equation is that it does not offer a substantial benefit for both sides, and therefore does not inspire universal confidence. What was finally agreed upon was conditional amnesty. Firstly, the victims of apartheid should have the opportunity to tell what happened to them, and for their sufferings to be publicly acknowledged. Secondly, the perpetrators of political crimes should account for their deeds by making full and truthful disclosure of their actions. Lastly, reparations should be made to the victims.

President Mandela, in consultation with his cabinet, appointed the members of the Commission. Public nominations were called for and interviews held, after which the president decided on the final appointees. . . .

The Commission had a complex structure. Separate committees were appointed, one on Human Rights Violations, another on Amnesty, and a third on Reparation and Rehabilitation, while a Research Department investigated human rights' violations and played a crucial role in drawing up the detailed five-volume report, which the TRC [Truth and Reconciliation Commission] published in October 1998.

The Commission was required to investigate "the conflicts of the past," and the first volume of its report did provide a general historical context to the events it investigated. . . . Its life was to be only two years, for it was thought that the Commission's work should be completed before the second democratic elections, due in mid-1999. Yet, there were far more amnesty applications than had been expected and the amnesty hearings continued into 2000.

Sonia G. Benson, Nancy Matuszak, and Meghan
Appel O'Meara, eds., History Behind the Headlines:
The Origins of Conflicts Worldwide, *vol. 2. Detroit:*
Gale, 2001, pp. 257–258.

An important aspect of the amnesty process is the stipulation that the life of the TRC be prescribed, on the grounds that a time frame would provide an incentive for perpetrators wishing to come forward and, after making full disclosure, to be amnistied. Failure to take advantage of the process within the prescribed time would open perpetrators to prosecution in the ordinary courts of law.

Publicly Acknowledging the Past

During the hearings held by the TRC, harrowing stories of suffering and cruelty were heard. Did the process result in reconciliation?

One strong criticism of the amnesty process is that it frustrates justice and the desire for punishment. This does not take into account the fact that many of the recipients of amnesty experience a kind of punishment they never anticipated: the shame of being publicly exposed. The exposure of their participation in despicable acts of cruelty has in some cases resulted in broken families, disorientation and loss of self-esteem—a form of punishment that can arguably be far more devastating than that exacted by an ordinary jail sentence. Equally, the contrition leading to a plea for forgiveness, as part of a quest for reacceptance in society, can be far more restorative than the hoped-for rehabilitative effects of an ordinary prison term. The cure in the method of the TRC is located within social practice rather than in the artificiality of punitive isolation. This experience raises legitimate questions about traditional methods of retributive justice.

It can be said that as a result of the TRC, South Africa has become a more sensitive and a more complex society. South Africans have been forced to confront the complex contradictions of the human condition, and the need to devise adequate social arrangements to deal with them. The healing that results will not be instant. It will come from the new tendency for South Africans to be willing to negotiate their way through social, intellectual, religious, political and cultural diversity. In sum, it will come from the progressive accumulation of ethical and moral insights.

Certainly, some objectives have been achieved. No South African, particularly white South Africans, can ever claim ignorance of how apartheid disrupted and destroyed the lives of millions of black people in the name of the white electorate. All South Africans can now claim to have a common base of knowledge about where they have come from, particularly in the last 50 years, and this is an essential foundation for the emergence of a new national value system. Public acknowledgment of South Africa's history of racism represents a form of reconciliation.

South African Archbishop Desmond Tutu (seated center) listens to testimony from witnesses during a Truth and Reconciliation Commission meeting on April 15, 1996. © Oryx Media Archive/Gallo Images/Getty Images.

Moving Toward Social Justice

The TRC has not by any means been a smooth process. Many whites, particularly among Afrikaners, felt that the TRC was a punitive witch-hunt, targeting them as a community. This criticism did not take into account the fact that the TRC also addressed gross human rights violations perpetrated by the liberation movements themselves. The even-handedness of the TRC in this regard is very clear in its report, and could itself be regarded as a significant contribution to reconciliation.

There are people who are not happy with the amnesty mechanism and strongly feel that justice has been compromised. Fortunately, a negotiated transition ensured there were functioning institutions in place for citizens to exercise their rights.

Reconciliation is not a single event. It is a process. The TRC was a mechanism to deal with enormous human tensions which could have exploded with devastating consequences. It enabled South Africans to navigate successfully through very rough seas.

Mandela, 20 Years On: Change, But for Whom?

Pusch Commey

In the following viewpoint, Pusch Commey contends that although many things have improved for blacks in South Africa since Nelson Mandela's 1990 release from prison, economic apartheid remains a fact of life. While a large percentage of blacks now rule politics, a small percentage of whites still rule the economics. Commey writes that 95 percent of the economy is owned by white South Africa. The improvements in black lives are superficial, he argues, and have little relation to the net worth of blacks or to their involvement in the economy. The wealth created circulates among whites while shared poverty and debt circulate among blacks. Commey does not envision much change over the next twenty years. Commey is a Johannesburg, South Africa–based attorney, writer, and the South African correspondent for New African *magazine.*

It was the moment the world had been waiting for. A moment of truth. A free Mandela meant a free world. An act of exorcism of an evil spirit called apartheid that would set black and white South Africa free. On 11 February 1990, he walked out of the Victor Vester Prison in Cape Town, hand in hand with his

Pusch Commey, "Mandela, 20 Years On: Change, But for Whom?," *New African*, March 2010. Copyright © 2010 by Al Bawaba Ltd. All rights reserved. Reproduced by permission.

then wife, Winnie Mandela. The world waited to welcome him as their messiah.

When the history of South Africa is retold, one can conveniently calculate the years from BM (Before the release of Mandela) and AM (After the release of Mandela). Such is the significance of his triumph 27 years after his incarceration in 1963. At the Rivonia trial in the same year, apartheid judges would of course find him guilty of terrorism and various trumped-up charges. They had the power to impose the death sentence. Mandela told them in their face that he was prepared to die for his ideal of a free South Africa. Perhaps sensing martyrdom, they chose to imprison him for life.

There have been analyses upon analyses as to why the formidable apartheid regime chose to negotiate itself out of power. It had little choice. Apartheid was a festering wound that was going to get worse with each passing day.

Already in the 1980s all the vestiges of this monumental human injustice was falling apart at the seams. Mass protests orchestrated by the United Democratic Front, the proxy of the exiled African National Congress, were paralysing the nation. Already the Group Areas Act that separated black and white was no longer enforceable as black South Africans slowly found their way into white areas.

The overstretched security forces had lost their willpower. Bantustans created by the white overlords were not viable. The international community was becoming more strident, angrily calling for sanctions. The country was becoming more and more ungovernable, and the interdependence of black and white along the labour and business fronts respectively meant that separate development was a delusion.

Historical events also expedited apartheid's demise. While the Cold War between the West and East lasted, it was convenient for the apartheid regime to claim to be fighting communism. But with the fall of the Berlin Wall and the implosion of the Soviet Union, that cover was blown. Not to mention another moment of truth, when the much-vaunted apartheid army was soundly thrashed in Angola by Cuban forces and the MPLA at the famous battle of Cuito Cuanavale. Namibia's independence from South Africa followed in 1990 and South Africa's was not far behind.

Perhaps when the major banks abroad called in their loans to the South African government, the regime, hit in the pocket, had no choice but to close shop. Bankrupt Apartheid sorely needed a liquidator. But who would carry the white cross? F.W. de Klerk, the man who had the courage to call it a day, explains why apartheid did not work.

> The whites wanted too much land for themselves—they did not make the offer too attractive enough. Secondly, we, the different races, became economically interdependent, because of economic growth. Actually, we became an omelette. Thirdly, and maybe the most important reason, is that the majority of the blacks felt that, that was not how they wanted their political rights. So we admitted to ourselves that we had failed and we had to devise a new vision that would ensure justice for all.

Noble words, but not the whole truth.

Die Groot Krokodil (the big crocodile) P.W. Botha, prime minister from 1978–1984 and executive president from 1984–1989, started the liquidation process. When he gave his "crossing the Rubicon speech" in 1985, the expectation was that the moribund apartheid policy would end. The Big Crocodile, however, developed cold feet. Instead, he sought to place conditions on Mandela for his freedom, seeking to wrest the moral high ground from him. Either Mandela renounced violence, thereby breaking ranks with the ANC, or refused to renounce violence, thereby confirming his commitment to "terrorism" and the justification for his continued incarceration.

Mandela rejected the offer. In his reply, read out at a mass rally in Soweto by his daughter Zindzi, then a teenager, he refused to negotiate his freedom and pledged to the people that his freedom was inextricably linked to theirs.

When P.W. Botha had a stroke in January 1989, he stubbornly clung to power, until he was pushed out by his successor F.W. de Klerk, who started a chain of events that culminated in the unconditional release of Mandela. Before then, there had been several contracts between the ANC, managed by the revered Oliver Tambo, and the apartheid regime, as well as several top level meetings with Mandela himself.

The events that unfolded after his release and the subsequent unbanning of all liberation movements are well documented. To his credit, F.W. de Klerk, in one fell swoop, unravelled everything and convinced the fearful whites that he was in control of the political process. It was simply the right thing to do. Up to this day, there are right-wingers who see him as a traitor.

After the momentous February 11 release, negotiations after negotiations followed between all parties, interspersed with violence, leading to a new constitution and the first multi-racial elections on April 27, 1994. De Klerk and Mandela shared the Nobel Peace Prize in 1993 but even that has been contentious as De Klerk was seen as backing Mangosuthu Buthelezi's Zulu-based Inkatha Freedom Party in a low-intensity war against the ANC that claimed several hundred black lives in the run-up to negotiations—an action calculated to weaken the ANC.

Change, But for Whom?

Twenty years, how is South Africa doing? Politically, it has a thriving democracy, with one of the finest constitutions on the planet. There have been regular elections every five years. Democracy has taken root amidst the rule of law. The contestation for power within and without political parties rages democratically with occasional fireworks. Gradually, South Africa has become a normal country where blacks and whites engage freely, even though racial undercurrents simmer.

Some psychological scarring and trauma remain among blacks, although for whites, who have been freed from their demons, it is a breath of fresh air, especially when Armageddon

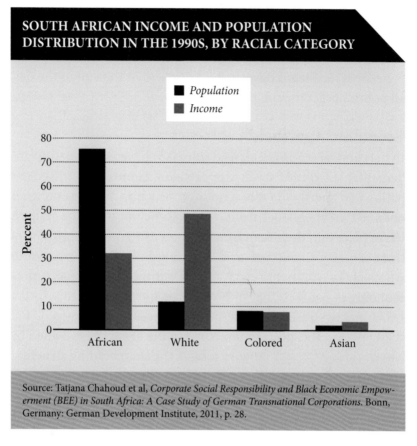

SOUTH AFRICAN INCOME AND POPULATION DISTRIBUTION IN THE 1990S, BY RACIAL CATEGORY

Source: Tatjana Chahoud et al, *Corporate Social Responsibility and Black Economic Empowerment (BEE) in South Africa: A Case Study of German Transnational Corporations.* Bonn, Germany: German Development Institute, 2011, p. 28.

did not happen as they had feared. The country has remained fairly prosperous and well managed by a black government such that it is often said that whites have never had it so good—shedding their erstwhile pariah status and becoming accepted into the community of nations, with expanded business opportunities. Today, ironically, white South Africa is more popular in other African countries than a black South Africa bristling with xenophobia.

With all the major economic pillars of the country firmly in white hands, the black majority has had to rely on the government to save their economic souls. It has not been easy. A sophisticated "First World" system built on the back of cheap black labour was only going to be sustained by a well-educated populace. This had to be accelerated amidst the tensions that came with continued white resistance on the economic front—80% of blacks rule the politics, 10% of whites rule the economics. Economic dominance was facilitated by apartheid politics. At the end of the day, all politics boil down to bread.

Economic Apartheid

In the euphoria of political freedom, many have forgotten the fundamental reason for slavery, oppression, subjugation, discrimination and apartheid—the economic. Much as African countries obtained independence from their colonial masters, the systems left in place and their management has ensured that wealth from these countries continue to flow upwards to the North. South Africa is the continent's economic powerhouse but the size of its economy is equal to that of Finland or the State of Ohio in the USA. Its huge reserves of natural resources, however, feeds the West. Within this powerhouse, 95% of the economy is owned by white South Africa. A cursory look at the shareholding structure on the Johannesburg Stock Exchange will reveal that blacks are not dining. Only a few politically blessed ones have their noses in there. Then there is kith and kin economics practised by the big companies in Europe and America who command big slices of the shareholding of major South African companies.

Another look at the juicy bits of the economy reveal distressing realities—80% of blacks occupy less than 20% of professions, be it lawyers, accountants or doctors. In business, blacks hang on to the fringes. There is a disturbing absence of blacks in the value chain of most businesses. Huge numbers work the bottom as hewers of wood. No wonder the trickle-down effect has been huge squalid informal settlements in the midst of opulence. Any threat of changing the situation is met with threats of capital flight back to the North and job losses for the wretched.

So why is economic apartheid not being fought as vigorously as political apartheid? Part of the reason may be the free market system that rules the world, weighted in favour of race, warts and all. Whose money and network ensures that a race will remain at the top of the food chain? It is so with South Africa. Property rights was the most important concern of whites as part of the negotiated settlement to a new South Africa. It is enshrined in the constitution. So the tinkering goes on endlessly 20 years after Mandela's physical freedom, ensuring that 84% of the country's land remains with 10% whites.

Successes

Some successes have been cited with respect to improvements in black lives. Millions of South Africans get their basic water needs satisfied for free. The number of households with electricity has shot up from 50% to 80%. The banking system has expanded to embrace the black underclass—63% of the population have bank accounts as against 45% 20 years ago. And 86% of households have mobile phones. There is an expanding black middle class. Most of these improvements, however, are cosmetic. They have little relation to the net worth of blacks or black participation in the economy.

The catch is, all this good news comes from a growing economy that has expanded black consumers and debtors but not black owners of the factors of production and black creditors. The wealth that is created is not circulating among blacks. Shared poverty and debt is! Thus South Africa has become the world champion of inequalities, overtaking Brazil in the process. Education is on the decline in black areas with deteriorating results. The achievement of distinctions in Matric Exams (after 11 years of education) is overwhelmingly white. Most whites can afford to attend the best schools and secure the best tuition.

The official unemployment rate is 30%, and overwhelmingly black. What is more, 5.7 million South Africans are HIV-positive, out of a population of 48 million, and the 5.7 million is made up of mostly black people, burdening a creaking public health system. Most whites enjoy medical insurance in first-rate hospitals.

A woman walks with a bucket for water in a Johannesburg, South Africa, squatter camp in 2010. Millions of people who migrate to urban areas in search of work only end up unemployed in such camps. © Per-Anders Pettersson/Getty Images.

Stomachs First

The question remains—20 years from today, will economic apartheid be defeated? Will there be the same local and international support for the eradication of economic apartheid? South Africa will need another Mandela. The political one is heading for the sunset, sadly the economic one is nowhere on the horizon.

Interestingly, black people with political power in South Africa have not shown the same kind of zeal. It has been a case of stomach first. There has been a flourish of hungry political entrepreneurs who have given birth to "tenderpreneurs." Access to political power has bestowed the right to give huge government tenders and contracts to friends and relatives with no capacity to execute. Such tenders are simply subcontracted, mostly to white companies with the capacity to deliver. Conversely, huge kickbacks are received. It is taxpayer's money that blacks feed on, not the creation of value in the marketplace. And the politicians preside over this distribution with the "me first" mantra. Public servants have taken the cue, running side-businesses related to their sphere of influence. No wonder inequalities in South Africa are found not only among the races but between blacks as well. And where does that leave the ordinary black? In hell?

There has been talk about the nationalisation of mines, spearheaded by the vociferous leader of the ANC Youth League, Julius Malema. At 28 years of age, his bulging waistline and lavish lifestyle belies his roots. Susan Shabangu, the outspoken minister of mines, has declared that such nationalisation will not occur in her lifetime. Some ANC bigwigs find the topic uncomfortable, including the South African Communist Party, an alliance partner of the ANC. In all this, the president of the country, Jacob Zuma, stays mum.

BEE Dead?

So whatever happened to Black Economic Empowerment (BEE) or Broad Based Black Economic Empowerment (BBBEE)? Most analysts have declared it dead, successfully done in by those who had the most to gain. The strategy has been co-option. Political power has been corrupted such that few are prepared to rise up against economic injustice. Of course, the Dom Perignon and Jack Daniels taste far better than the rural brew. Life in Soweto is not as comfortable as in the leafy suburbs of Sandton!

Black Economic Empowerment has merely become an insurance scheme for growing white capital, where blacks who can politically rock the boat are co-opted to boards, shares, white privileges, and golf.

Perhaps in 20 years' time, there will still be many policy documents of black empowerment, fine speeches, and fine whisky. The downtrodden will remain trodden. Come election time, the same politicians will trudge through the mud to the downtrodden's godforsaken settlements to plead for their votes. Of course, they will get them—under a shower of promises. Once in a while there will be the distraction of big events. And life goes on. The more things change, the more they remain the same.

CHAPTER 3

Personal Narratives

Chapter Exercises

1. Writing Prompt

Imagine you are a nonwhite teenager in apartheid South Africa. Write a one-page journal entry describing the differences between your lifestyle and that of a white South African.

2. Group Activity

Form groups and develop five interview questions that can be used in conducting oral histories of political prisoners serving time in Robben Island prison.

A South African Reflects on His Childhood

Christian S. Gerber

In the following viewpoint, Christian S. Gerber shares his experiences growing up in South Africa. He relates that his family was poor and tells how he sold produce from the family farm. He shares that the only black people he saw when he was young were men working on the roads and talks about the ways in which their culture differed from that of the whites. He voices the opinion that a person had to live in South Africa to understand the white perception of blacks. He explains that in South Africa the only political viewpoint accepted was survival, and that whites believed that black rule meant the end of the whites. Gerber served as a senior manager for three of South Africa's major banks. In 1995 he relocated his family to the United States, where he opened his own business in Alabama.

We lived in a society of predominantly white people. There were a few colored families living in the area and they were all working as gardeners or house cleaners for the white people. I never understood that really as a child, and really did not have much time to worry about it either. I attended the only primary school in the immediate area and only white children went there. We always believed that there was a school for colored children a few miles away, but I never saw it. Most of the colored children living in [the village of] Olifantshoek never went to school as far as I could tell. The colored people called the whites "baas" and "mies" which was like "boss" and "madam". We in turn called the men "outa" which was a respectful "old man" or the women "aia" which is a word for an adult woman. First names were very seldom used and were always preceded by one of these adjectives. . . .

Some of them were big friends of ours. We played games together and hunted (mostly birds) together. Although they acted in a subjective way, they were never slaves. They had freedom to come and go as they please. The only relationship they had with the white people was that of employer and employee. . . .

Life on a Poor Farm

Our lives were about surviving as poor people and yes, we recognized that there were others even poorer and less fortunate than ourselves. We treated those people with the same respect as we did those who were more privileged, although we had less admiration for them.

I had my own vegetable garden. Although I was not even a teenager yet, I often had to help my dad in cultivating the fields where we grew sweet potatoes, potatoes, pumpkin and various other vegetables.

So, I got my own piece of garden to plant and sold all the produce to the colored people. They were eager to buy from me because my products were fresh out of the garden and inexpensive. We were not taught to be greedy and rip other people off and so we had no reason to feel guilty about any trading deal.

Observing Black Culture

We lived in an area where there were no black ethnic groups. The only times we ever saw black people, when we saw groups of men working on the roads. These were people who helped with the upkeep of the gravel roads.

They did not speak our language. They appeared very unfriendly and we were scared of them. We could not communicate with them and we did not trust them. In fact, there was never any opportunity to build any kind of friendship or trusting relationship.

They must have seen us as occupants of their country and would not have understood our side of the story. Our culture was very different to theirs and so there was no common bond or interest anywhere.

They had their own beliefs and practices. No churches and only witchdoctors. It took many years before any of them were ever converted to our faith and beliefs, but even those remained different in their own cultures and outlook on life. We had a Western, capitalistic culture and this was foreign to Africa. We believed in a one-woman-one-man marriage relationship, but in Africa a man's wealth was often counted in the number of wives he possessed. Young ladies were traded by their fathers for a dowry (normally a number of cattle) to a husband she may never have loved—something completely unheard of in our custom. The women were in subjection to the men and even if a man would mistreat his wife, she would not dare to leave him as this would bring reproach on her family.

We believed that the black people had very little respect for human life. This scary thought became more real when TV came to South Africa and we had the opportunity to witness some of the cruelties that they would inflict upon one another. What is even worse is the fact that the news media often helped to incite these actions. Young children enjoyed the media attention and would go to the extreme to get the cameras focused on them.

It sounds cruel to describe the culture amongst the black people in Africa in a derogative way, but one needs to have lived there to understand some of these perceptions. There are numerous ethnic groups of which the Xhosa, Zulu, Sotho, Tswana,

Venda and Ndebele were the biggest and most prominent groups. Many of these groups have always treated the others with some mistrust and groups like the Xhosas and Zulus have never lived in peace with one another. It was probably this division amongst them that gave the white people the opportunity to rule this land.

The arrival of the white man with a different culture just added more oil to a proverbial fire. . . .

Apartheid Protected White South Africans

It was later in my school career that I learned more of the struggles between white and black. Sure, I learned the white man's viewpoint and history as written by the white man, but even today I still do not find it all that strange. Whenever there are opposite parties involved in life situation, there will always be two sides of the same story told. . . .

I learned about the difference in cultures. I learned about wars and struggles for land and power. I learned very little about political viewpoints. In fact, we basically accepted only one political viewpoint; namely "survival".

So in South Africa, it was always either the black people or the white people. There was never a nation under one flag or under one God. We believed that if the black people would rule, it would mean the end of the whites.

A Political Prisoner Serves Time on Robben Island

Mac Maharaj

In the following viewpoint, activist Mac Maharaj shares his experiences as a political prisoner in apartheid South Africa. He describes the scene as he and five others were transported in a small compartment of a closed truck to Robben Island prison and talks about their suspicions of one prisoner. He tells what happened once they arrive at Robben Island, what prison conditions were like, and how the prisoners organized. He goes on to explain how they conspired to help fellow prisoner Nelson Mandela write his autobiography and smuggle it out of prison. Maharaj was an antiapartheid activist, political prisoner, and negotiator in the South African constitutional talks. He served as minister of transport in South Africa's first democratic government and was an editorial consultant for the book Mandela: The Authorized Portrait.

On Sunday morning, 3 January 1965, [African National Congress (ANC) member] Laloo Chiba and I are herded into a small compartment of a closed prison truck at Leeuwkop Prison. We are barefoot, dressed in khaki prison shorts and short-sleeved shirts. A third prisoner, Raymond Nyanda, joins

Mac Maharaj, *Reflections in Prison: Voices from the South African Liberation Struggle.* Amherst: University of Massachusetts Press, 2002, pp. x–xii. Copyright © 2002 by the University of Massachusetts Press. All rights reserved. Reproduced by permission.

us. He is wearing a prison jersey, a white canvas bunny jacket, prison socks and shoes. Soft spoken, shining skin and none of that harassed, unkempt look of the usual prisoner. Three other prisoners join us. We are put into leg irons and handcuffed in pairs. My ankle is locked to the ankle brace of the right leg of my partner; handcuffs attach my left wrist to his right wrist.

The compartment, separated from the driver's cab and the back of the truck, has seating space for four. It is intended for warders when they ride shotgun, accompanying prisoners packed into the back of the truck. The six of us have standing room only and take turns to rest on the seats. The contortions we have to get through to effect this shuffling around must have been the inspiration for the Rubik's cube. Our truck is escorted by a van containing warders. Also escorting us is a sedan car in which Brigadier Aucamp, the head of prison security, is travelling with his wife and daughter, presumably a family holiday reimbursed as escort duty allowance.

Meeting a Suspicious Prisoner

Our attempts to protest against our conditions are stifled. Each prisoner is locked in thought. Something doesn't fit. How is it that Raymond Nyanda has clean clothes, shoes, socks, a jersey and a canvas jacket? He breaks the silence, introduces himself; claims he is a political prisoner who was a reporter in Durban [South Africa] for the *Sunday Times*. His brother-in-law, he tells us, is Leslie Messina. Leslie, we know, is living in exile in Swaziland. He was the general secretary of the South African Congress of Trade Unions (SACTU). Already in my mind there lurks the idea that from prison we may be able to communicate with Leslie through Raymond. Some of the others begin to question him. It is becoming an interrogation. Suspicion churns through my mind. I must ward off an interrogation. We must not arouse Raymond's suspicions. We need to find ways of establishing whether he is a plant and what his mission is. The trip becomes nerve-racking. We are unable to talk freely, share experiences and bond as freedom fighters.

Prisoners are forced to perform menial tasks such as breaking rocks and sewing clothes at Robben Island Prison in 1964. © Express/Archive Photos/Getty Images.

We reach Robben Island on 5 January. Laloo, Raymond, [ANC member] Andrew Masondo and I are taken to the "segregation" section of the prison. This is where our leaders are being kept in single cells after the Rivonia Trial. We are about 40 prisoners in this section. Smoking is a punishable offence in prison, but we begin to notice that Raymond, though he does not smoke, has access to tobacco. He courts the friendship of one of our comrades. He gives him a Parker ballpoint pen as a present. Our leadership is convinced that Raymond has been put among us to spy. We talk to him but treat him with reserve.

What tempts a man—a black man in apartheid South Africa—to sell his soul? We conclude that he is in prison for fraud and has probably been promised a shortened sentence and an easy life in prison. His prison card states that he is serving a six-year sentence for a political offence. A few months later we are working at the lime quarry with picks and shovels. The prison commander drives over and loudly calls for Raymond. Within earshot he says, "Raymond, you have won your appeal and your sentence has been shortened. Come along, you are being released." Exit Raymond Nyanda. Mission accomplished or mission failed? Months later we get hold of a smuggled copy of the *Financial Mail*. We find a snippet of news in it: Raymond Nyanda, financial adviser to a Soweto [South African township] tycoon, has committed suicide.

Organizing in Secret

We begin to organise ourselves in prison. We demand the right to study. We are granted the privilege to study by correspondence provided we can pay for the course. We do not have a single shelf, desk or chair in our cells. After a year we are granted a single bookshelf and counter without a chair or bench. Later we get benches.

Conditions in prison are harsh and the rules are stringent. Any abuse of our study privilege could lead to its withdrawal. Contraventions of prison regulations are punished harshly and summarily. The punishments: denial of meals, spare diet for up to 42 days, lashes and even additional prison sentences.

We organise ourselves by fair means or foul. We are denied all news of the outside world. We smuggle newspapers, journals and books. At one stage we get hold of a pocket radio. We are not allowed to smoke. We smuggle tobacco. We are not allowed to talk among ourselves. We defy this rule until the authorities are unable to enforce it. We are kept separate from the bulk of the political prisoners. We set up a clandestine committee charged with devising ways to communicate with them. Our cells are raided. We find ways to conceal our communications and our smuggled books. We make a false compartment in a bench. We turn a piece of rusted metal into a set of keys to open the prison locks, including the master lock.

Much of this is done in strict secrecy—not even our fellow prisoners are in the know. Everything clandestine that we do is carried out under the strictest discipline and on the basis of the need to know.

Our lifeline is news of the world outside prison: the welfare of our loved ones and friends, the struggle within the country, the activities of the movement in exile and the solidarity action of the world at large. We monitor minutely every snippet of information we can get hold of, mull over its significance. We make the world our own. We follow the developments and progress of humankind's struggle in every corner of the world.

Each of us buries his pain in the pain of our loved ones. We fume and fret about them, and we subsume their travails in the struggle to overthrow apartheid. We grit our teeth, steel ourselves and arm ourselves in every possible way to continue the struggle until freedom reigns. Surrender is unthinkable. Death or victory became our watchwords.

Smuggling Mandela's Autobiography out of Prison

My release date is creeping up on me. Towards the end of 1975 [South African activist Ahmed] "Kathy" Kathrada broaches the idea that [Nelson] Mandela should write his autobiography. Mandela, [ANC Youth League founder Walter] Sisulu, Kathrada and I discuss the proposal. My release, which is due at the end of 1976, would give us an opportunity to smuggle the manuscript out of prison. It is an enormous challenge. Can we pull it off? First, there is the writing. Mandela will have to write purely from memory. Then there is the secrecy. He cannot indulge in the luxury of keeping his notes in his cell. Whatever he writes each night must be out of his hands the next morning. He has no access to reference works. Conditions require that when he sits to write at night he will not have access to what he has already written. And how shall we get the manuscript out safely?

We maintain the utmost secrecy in writing the autobiography because the authorities are likely to impose summary and collective punishment on the entire body of prisoners. We fear divisions among ourselves should this happen, both between the different political organisations, and possibly even among our own organisation's members, especially if the authorities were to withdraw our study privileges. We are mindful of the critical role of the privilege to study in enabling most of us to maintain our sanity in this harsh and brutal environment.

We plan to execute the project in a concentrated burst. We have to plan for the fact that, even though I shall only be due for release on 17 December 1976, the authorities might descend on me at any time, months before my release date, and whisk me away from Robben Island, thereby unwittingly preventing the smuggling of the manuscript.

We would have to transcribe the manuscript from Mandela's handwriting into a fine tiny handwriting on a daily basis. Mandela's original version would end up with Kathrada, who would be responsible for concealing it in prison. The transcribed version, written in a form suitable for concealment and smuggling out of prison, became my responsibility. We drew Laloo Chiba into the team.

Mandela started writing in January 1976. He wrote an average of 10 to 15 pages a night. Within three months he had completed the task. We had worked faster than we had planned. It was better to be early than to be caught by my premature removal from Robben Island.

We convinced ourselves that we had devised means of concealment that would escape detection. It was the first time we would be smuggling out such a large quantity of written material.

An Imprisoned ANC Leader Learns About Soweto and the New Activists

Nelson Mandela

In the following viewpoint, an excerpt from his autobiography, revered South African statesman Nelson Mandela talks about the 1976 student uprising in Soweto and the young men who took part in it. He explains how he and his fellow political prisoners first heard about the uprising and then shares what they found out from the young men imprisoned for participating in it. The young prisoners, Mandela concludes, are unlike any others he has seen before. He states his amazement at their behavior in prison and offers examples of their reactions to prison regulations. He goes on to discuss the young revolutionaries and their black consciousness movement, which he considers more a philosophy than a movement. Mandela led the struggle to replace South Africa's apartheid regime with a multiracial democracy. A longtime African National Congress leader, he was a Nobel Peace Prize winner and former president of South Africa.

As diligent as we were in gathering news and information, our knowledge of current events was always sketchy.

Nelson Mandela, *Long Walk to Freedom: The Autobiography of Nelson Mandela*. New York: Little, Brown, 1994, pp. 420–423. From *Long Walk To Freedom* by Nelson Mandela. Copyright © 1994, 1995 by Nelson Rolihlahla Mandela. By permission of Little, Brown and Company. All rights reserved.

Happenings in the outside world were muffled by the fact that we heard of them first through rumor; only later might they be confirmed by a newspaper account or an outside visitor.

The Soweto Uprising

In June of 1976, we began to hear vague reports of a great uprising in the country. The whispers were fanciful and improbable: the youth of Soweto had overthrown the military and the soldiers had dropped their guns and fled. It was only when the first young prisoners who had been involved in the June 16 uprising began to arrive on Robben Island in August that we learned what truly happened.

On June 16, 1976, fifteen thousand schoolchildren gathered in Soweto to protest the government's ruling that half of all classes in secondary schools must be taught in Afrikaans. Students did not want to learn and teachers did not want to teach in the language of the oppressor. Pleadings and petitions by parents and teachers had fallen on deaf ears. A detachment of police confronted this army of earnest schoolchildren and without warning opened fire, killing thirteen-year-old Hector Pieterson and many others. The children fought with sticks and stones, and mass chaos ensued, with hundreds of children wounded, and two white men stoned to death.

The events of that day reverberated in every town and township of South Africa. The uprising triggered riots and violence across the country. Mass funerals for the victims of state violence became national rallying points. Suddenly the young people of South Africa were fired with the spirit of protest and rebellion. Students boycotted schools all across the country. ANC [African National Congress] organizers joined with students to actively support the protest. Bantu Education had come back to haunt its creators, for these angry and audacious young people were its progeny.

New Prisoners Arrive

In September, the isolation section was filled with young men who had been arrested in the aftermath of the uprising. Through whispered conversations in an adjacent hallway we learned firsthand what had taken place. My comrades and I were enormously cheered; the spirit of mass protest that had seemed dormant through the 1960s was erupting in the 1970s. Many of these young people had left the country to join our own military movement, and then smuggled themselves back home. Thousands of them were trained in our camps in Tanzania, Angola, and Mozambique. There is nothing so encouraging in prison as learning that the people outside are supporting the cause for which you are inside.

These young men were a different breed of prisoner than we had ever seen before. They were brave, hostile, and aggressive; they would not take orders, and shouted "*Amandla!*" [Power!] at every opportunity. Their instinct was to confront rather than cooperate. The authorities did not know how to handle them, and they turned the island upside down. During the [1963–1964] Rivonia [sabotage and conspiracy] Trial, I remarked to a security policeman that if the government did not reform itself, the freedom fighters who would take our place would someday make the authorities yearn for us. That day had indeed come on Robben Island.

In these young men we saw the angry revolutionary spirit of the times. I had had some warning. At a visit with [my wife] Winnie a few months before, she had managed to tell me through our coded conversation that there was a rising class of discontented youth who were militant and Africanist in orientation. She said they were changing the nature of the struggle and that I should be aware of them.

Refusing to Conform

The new prisoners were appalled by what they considered the barbaric conditions of the island, and said they could not understand how we could live in such a way. We told them that they should have seen the island in 1964. But they were almost as skeptical of us as they were of the authorities. They chose to ignore our calls for discipline and thought our advice feeble and unassertive.

Nelson Mandela visits his former cell at Robben Prison in 1994. © Jurgen Schadeberg/Getty Images.

It was obvious that they regarded us, the Rivonia Trialists, as moderates. After so many years of being branded a radical revolutionary, to be perceived as a moderate was a novel and not altogether pleasant feeling. I knew that I could react in one of two ways: I could scold them for their impertinence or I could listen to what they were saying. I chose the latter.

When some of these men, such as Strini Moodley of the South African Students' Organization and Saths Cooper of the Black People's Convention, came into our section, I had them give us papers on their movement and philosophy. I wanted to know what had brought them to the struggle, what motivated them, what their ideas were for the future.

Shortly after their arrival on the island, the commanding officer came to me and asked me as a favor to address the young men. He wanted me to tell them to restrain themselves, to recognize the fact that they were in prison and to accept the discipline of prison life. I told him that I was not prepared to do that. Under the circumstances, they would have regarded me as a collaborator of the oppressor.

These fellows refused to conform to even basic prison regulations. One day I was at the Head Office conferring with the commanding officer. As I was walking out with the major, we came upon a young prisoner being interviewed by a prison official. The young man, who was no more than eighteen years old, was wearing his prison cap in the presence of senior officers, a violation of regulations. Nor did he stand up when the major entered the room, another violation.

The major looked at him and said, "Please, take off your cap." The prisoner ignored him. Then in an irritated tone, the major said, "Take off your cap." The prisoner turned and looked at the major, and said, "What for?"

I could hardly believe what I had just heard. It was a revolutionary question: What for? The major also seemed taken aback, but managed a reply. "It is against regulations," he said. The young prisoner responded, "Why do you have this regulation? What is the purpose of it?" This questioning on the part of the prisoner was too much for the major, and he stomped out of the room, saying, "Mandela, you talk to him." But I would not intervene on his behalf, and simply bowed in the direction of the prisoner to let him know that I was on his side.

Analyzing the Black Consciousness Movement

This was our first exposure to the Black Consciousness Movement [BCM]. With the banning of the ANC, PAC [Pan Africanist Congress], and Communist Party, the Black Consciousness Movement helped fill a vacuum among young people. Black Consciousness was less a movement than a philosophy and grew out of the idea that blacks must first liberate themselves from the sense of psychological inferiority bred by three centuries of white rule. Only then could the people rise up in confidence and truly liberate themselves from repression. While the Black Consciousness Movement advocated a non-racial society, they excluded whites from playing a role in achieving that society.

These concepts were not unfamiliar to me: they closely mirrored ideas I myself held at the time of the founding of the ANC Youth League a quarter-century before. We, too, were Africanists; we, too, stressed ethnic pride and racial self-confidence; we, too, rejected white assistance in the struggle. In many ways, Black Consciousness represented the same response to the same problem that had never gone away.

But just as we had outgrown our Youth League outlook, I was confident that these young men would transcend some of the strictures of Black Consciousness. While I was encouraged by their militancy, I thought that their philosophy, in its concentration on blackness, was exclusionary, and represented an intermediate view that was not fully mature. I saw my role as an elder statesman who might help them move on to the more inclusive ideas of the Congress Movement. I knew also that these young men would eventually become frustrated because Black Consciousness offered no program of action, no outlet for their protest.

Although we viewed the ranks of the BCM as a fertile ground for the ANC, we did not attempt to recruit these men. We knew that this would alienate both them and the other parties on the island. Our policy was to be friendly, to take an interest, to compliment them on their achievements, but not to proselytize. If they came to us and asked questions we would answer them— and a great many of them did come to us with questions.

A White South African Teen Discovers Truths About His Country

Mark Abrahamson

In the following viewpoint, South African teen Mark Abrahamson explains that he grew up in a protected environment away from the turmoil and strife associated with apartheid. He talks about the propaganda put forth by the white government and the government restrictions on what was taught in the schools, both of which helped blind people to the truths of what was really going on. He discusses the changes that have begun to take place in South Africa and how they have affected him personally. His generation, states Abrahamson, is the bridge from the old South Africa to a new one, and he intends to take an active role in the transition. At the time this viewpoint was written, Abrahamson was a sixteen-year-old living with his parents in an all-white suburb of Cape Town.

I often think to myself. I'm just so lucky to have been at this end of the whole apartheid system, lucky to have been brought into the world which I was born into. Around here we've got television, we've got two cars in the garage, we're linked to the Internet we've got the hi-fi system. What would have happened if I had been on the other side? Would I still be the same kind of guy?

Living a Sheltered Life

The majority of South Africans were oppressed during the time of my upbringing, but I was in a very protected environment and was kept away from the violence and the atrocities that were being committed. I think a lot of people outside South Africa have this perception that it was so violent that someone was getting shot around every corner, but it wasn't like that in my area. I've never seen a man killed before, even though just twenty kilometers away in the townships, young kids were being subjected to some *oke* [guy] walking into their house and gunning their parents down.

There were just such strong barriers between our two environments. As a kid I remember being at parks in our area and thinking to myself, Now why is that black person there? He shouldn't be there. It wasn't because I had anything against that person; that was just the normal way it was. If you look at Cape Town, it's quite remarkable: You've got a relatively affluent core center, and right next to it, really right over here, you've got a lot of poverty and unhappiness in the townships. But it didn't seem like these problems were right here in Cape Town; it seemed very distant, almost as if it was in another African country somewhere.

The Apartheid Government Spreads Propaganda

We weren't just sheltered; there was also an active hiding of the truth, propaganda, by the apartheid government. They knew that if we were able to analyze the true situation, sooner or later we would have come to the conclusion that it was wrong. The government controlled the television stations, for example, and the news became a joke after a while because it was so propagandist. If there was any violence in the townships, it was blamed on African forces fighting each other and not on white government intervention, which is what it was.

You also didn't really hear about the ANC [African National Congress]. Whenever you did, it was through the news, "these people are messing up our land" kind of thing. And I hadn't seen

Three boys play on a segregated beach in Durban, South Africa, in 1986. Many white South Africans grew up unaware of the injustices and abuses of apartheid. © William F. Campbell/ Time & Life Pictures/Getty.

pictures of [antiapartheid activist Nelson] Mandela, because you weren't allowed to have a picture of him anywhere around. He was made out to be a scary, violent character. "If he ever comes out," the government told us, "it will be the end of South Africa; we'll be thrown into civil war." I remember when I finally saw him released from prison on TV, it consciously came to mind: Why'd they put that funny old man in prison for so long? What could he have done?

In school, too, we weren't being told the real picture of South Africa. In the private school I attended, the government told the teachers what textbook to work from and what to teach. Certain books, like African literature, were just not allowed, and if teachers were caught teaching them in a class, they would be fined or put in prison. I remember reading [British writer] Rudyard Kipling's books about African animals, but that's not really

African literature, is it? It was almost like we could've been at a school in England.

I think I picked up on the racial situation quite young, but the whole process of assessing the situation and then feeling guilty is something which I've had to come to terms with much more recently. I don't know what I would've done if I was in my twenties at the height of apartheid. I don't know if I would've actually stood up and said, "I think it's completely wrong, and this is what I'm going to do about it."

But things have changed. We weren't told the truth for so long, but now we're hearing it all. We're starting to hear about the brutal attacks on people, to see pictures like the one of three policemen with their feet on a black man that they killed like it's a trophy. I've been shocked by what's come out, but I think it's necessary to hear it. What happened in our past is a wound. If we don't first put antiseptic on the wound, if we don't dig up our skeletons, literally and figuratively, it's never going to heal properly.

South Africa Is in an Age of Rediscovery

There's an age of rediscovery in South Africa at the moment, of finding out what's really out there, of getting to know everyone who is living here and consciously trying to live in harmony. We're the generation that's the bridge from the previous South Africa to a new one. Therefore I think it's crucial to become involved in this transformation, so that you have the sense of actually making a difference.

At my school I'm very involved in an organization called Interact, which focuses on community work. On Freedom Day [a national holiday commemorating the country's first democratic elections] this year there was a walk organized through all the townships, just to make us more aware of the city. Interact made it public to our school. I was very interested because I hadn't spent a long stretch of time in a township or really seen what was going on there. You can see things on television, but to actually be there and meet the people, reality kind of hits you.

So I went on the walk, and I got to see at close quarters what you normally just see from the road. We had to walk through a lot of really bad conditions. We even saw this one squatter community built over a rubbish dump. It was eye-opening because where we live around here, it's fairly clean. Walking through these places, I thought to myself, The only reason I'm not here is because of my skin color, which I didn't even choose. I also noticed that most of the people in the townships were quite friendly, happy people. I was expecting a lot more anger and irritation, like, "Why are you walking here?" But they actually wanted to show us around.

Looking Toward the Future

There's a fear now, especially among the more paranoid whites, that we're moving from a white supremacy to a black one, that black people are going to come knocking on our door, saying, "We're gonna divide your house in two." But that isn't what's happening. It seems there's this incredible feeling of forgiveness on the part of black people. It's like, "You know these white people have been terrible to us, but we're just going to show them that we're not made of the same stuff." I think we must be quite thankful for this atmosphere because as far as I'm concerned, black people have every right to turn the whole thing around and say, "Three hundred years we've been under this oppression, now it's your turn for the next three hundred."

Some white people are leaving South Africa, but I have no intention of doing so. I think if I was to be scooped up and put in Europe or America, I would be able to survive, but I would be very homesick for South Africa. Not many people have the privilege to be living in a country that is changing so rapidly, and I feel quite proud of my land, and I know that I belong here. I see our future being a positive one. I would like to be able to look back on my youth and say to myself, I was, even in a small way, somehow part of this success.

A Human Being Died That Night: A South African Story of Forgiveness

Pumla Gobodo-Madikizela

In the following viewpoint, Pumla Gobodo-Madikizela, a former member of South Africa's Truth and Reconciliation Commission, describes incidents of apartheid-era violence that greatly affected her. She describes the chaos and violence surrounding her as a five-year-old living in the black township of Langa near Cape Town. The shootings, blood, and human death she witnessed have haunted her ever since. She goes on to share two other memories of traumatic events and her confused feelings about the incidents. Gobodo-Madikizela is a professor in the Department of Psychology at South Africa's University of Cape Town, a senior research professor at the University of the Free State in Bloemfontein in South Africa, and the author of several books and numerous papers.

I, like every black South African, have lived a life shaped by the violence and the memories of apartheid. I have three linked stories to share. . . .

The first time I witnessed a scene of violence, I was five.

On March 21, 1960, a remarkable event occurred that transformed the nature of the anti-apartheid struggle in South Africa.

Pumla Gobodo-Madikizela, *A Human Being Died That Night: A South African Story of Forgiveness.* Boston: Houghton Mifflin, 2003, pp. 6–12. By permission of Houghton Mifflin. All rights reserved.

That day several thousand black people gathered in the township of Sharpeville to protest the notorious pass laws requiring blacks to carry internal passports, thus totally regulating their lives. The police opened fire on the crowd, killing 69 and wounding 186, including women and children. Most of the victims were shot in the back while fleeing. The Sharpeville incident was followed by countrywide demonstrations in black townships, leading to more bloodshed. In the township of Langa, the carnage was worse than in Sharpeville. At least this is how I would remember the events that I witnessed as a little girl of five from behind the hedge of my mother's small garden of our tiny house at 69 Brinton Street.

My memory of the 1960 Langa violence is something I still find difficult to shake out of my mind. Yet its accuracy was tested in 1996 when, as a committee member on South Africa's Truth and Reconciliation Commission, I was forced to revisit the events in Langa Township. What I remembered was the commotion in the row of houses on my street—all replicas of the matchbox structure that was my home. Men I knew as fathers of the girls and boys I played with were running past looking frightened, jumping fences to be anywhere but in their own homes. These were men I referred to as "father," or "so-and-so's father." We never called them by their first names. These were the same fathers you would not want to catch you doing anything wrong in the streets, like playing outside in the dark. Countless times I had shared candy with their children, candy already in my mouth, or in theirs, split and broken into bits inside the mouth so that one, two, or three others could have whatever tiny piece could be shared. These were the men who brought us the candy, but now they were scared and running.

Men I had never seen in my home came out of the coal shed at the back of our house with blackened faces. Some came into the house, moving beds to hide under them, or in closets. Others wore what I later remembered as a look of defiance or impotent rage. My own father was nowhere in sight, and my mother, heavily pregnant with my youngest sister, Sesi, was frantically calling out to the neighbors to try to establish his whereabouts. To escape this chaos of men—scared and defiant men—running in and out of my home, I went outside. There I saw what they were all running away from. Army trucks that looked like huge monsters roamed the streets menacingly, some charging furiously over walkways and into the large field in front of our house to fire into scattered groups of people. Vaguely aware of my elder brother standing behind me, I was witnessing something I had until then never seen before: live shooting, blood, and human death. The image that I was to recall many years later was that of a street covered in blood and bodies lined up like cattle in a slaughterhouse.

The indelible mark left by this incident returned in a flash on June 16, 1976, when I learned that police had on that day massacred over five hundred black students involved in a peaceful march against the imposition of Afrikaans as a language of instruction. When the youthful uprising broke out into violent protest in the Cape Town townships in August of that year, the memory of those bodies, bloodied and dismembered, on Brinton Street sixteen years earlier cried out inside me. At Fort Hare University (which was later closed for the rest of the year), I packed my bags and with other students abandoned my studies to be part of the protests.

Twenty years later, when I was invited to join the Truth and Reconciliation Commission (TRC), I was shocked to learn that what in my memory was a "massacre" had been otherwise. According to archival records, one death had resulted from the police shootings in Langa.

What conclusions can be drawn from what is to me a still haunting discrepancy? How can what I remember so vividly turn out to be unconfirmed by reports of what happened on that day? Since the countrywide protest in 1960 had been organized by the Pan-African Congress (PAC), when the TRC was preparing for its first public hearing in April 1996, I interviewed leaders of

the PAC, including its president, Clarence Makwethu, more to straighten out what was irresolvable in my mind than to establish the truth for the records of the TRC. None of them could confirm what was so very clear in my memory, suggesting that my memory was wrong. Or *was* it? Can what was still so vividly alive in my memory be described simply as a misrepresentation of the facts, a reconstruction and exaggeration of events as they had happened? I asked myself, What does this tell us about remembering traumatic events?

I can only suggest that when the safe world of a child is shattered by the violent invasion of police, the intensity of the moment is something that the experience of a five-year-old cannot absorb. She lacks the psychological capacity to contain the brutality before her eyes, and certainly has no language with which to re-present the traumatic events. *Blood*, *bodies*, and *death* are the only meaningful words that capture the image of what she cannot truly articulate through language.

Here is my third story.

In 1990 I was lecturing in psychology at the University of Transkei. This was an interesting time in the nominally independent homeland of Transkei. Bantu Holomisa, fondly known as "The General," had recently become leader of Transkei after a bloodless coup. Following the release of Nelson Mandela from prison, Holomisa announced that he was lifting the ban on all political organizations in Transkei. This edict, along with other events in Transkei, angered the South African government, and there was an attempted coup to remove Holomisa from office. Most people at the time, myself included, had no doubt that the apartheid South African government was implicated in the coup attempt. On the day of the incident, all businesses, schools, and other institutions were officially closed. You could see groups of people throughout the city of Umtata, capital of Transkei, their eyes cast upward toward Holomisa's office on the eleventh floor of Botha Sigcau, the tallest building in that small city.

I joined one of the groups that had converged in the streets, watching as the violent drama was unfolding, hoping that whoever was South Africa's agent would not succeed in what he was trying to do. Gunfire echoed in the streets and over our heads, and the smoke and dust pouring from the windows of Botha Sigcau were visible signs of the battle being fought inside. Despite the fact that the action on the eleventh floor was intensifying, despite the fact that it was clear that people could be seriously injured, despite all of that, I was waiting for the moment when I would celebrate victory with those multitudes watching in the streets. The moment of victory did arrive. The officer who was leading the coup attempt, Captain Craig Duli, was "captured." There was jubilation throughout the streets of Umtata. My car was filled to the brim; soldiers perched wherever there was space, hoisting their R1 rifles in the air through the windows as I honked and drove in circles in a spirit of celebration. The soldiers in my car immediately composed a song about how Captain Duli, "puppet of the Boers," couldn't stop Holomisa.

As the true nature of the events emerged, and we heard how the mutilated body of Captain Duli had been thrown into the trunk of an army vehicle, and how he later either died of his wounds or was shot along with others who had sided with him, I realized that I had been party to the killing of another human being. I had knowingly participated in an incident that would certainly result in the taking of a life. In my mind the point was not whether I could have done anything to stop it or not, but simply that I had been there, celebrating.

This was not the end of my shame. In 1996, while serving on the TRC, I was asked by the head of the Eastern Cape branch of the commission, the Reverend Bongani Finca, to be part of the panel that was going to hold a public hearing in Umtata. Before the hearing, each person on the panel was assigned to "facilitate" the testimony of two or more witnesses who would be appearing before the TRC. On similar occasions in the past, when I was not involved in organizing a public hearing, I usually made a point of reading the summaries of the stories of witnesses, and tried whenever possible to meet before the hearing started with those whose testimonies I was assigned to lead. Now I was shocked to see the name of Mrs. Nontobeko Duli, widow of Captain Duli, on the list of people scheduled to testify in Umtata. I did not know how I could sit on a panel and hear her story when only a few years earlier I had celebrated the death of her husband. Here she was, a victim like many others whose stories of trauma I had listened to. How could I with honesty convey words of comfort without first addressing my shame and guilt for having celebrated her husband's death? At the hearing in Umtata, Mrs. Duli was called to the witness stand, and she spoke about her loss, her children, and how she was struggling without the support of her husband. Her pain was as real to me as the rapid beating of my heart.

Glossary

African National Congress (ANC) Major South African political party founded in 1912 as a black nationalist movement.

Africans Term used in South Africa during apartheid to refer to black indigenous people.

Afrikaans Language derived chiefly from Dutch and developed in South Africa by its white residents.

Amandla South African political slogan calling for power to the black population.

apartheid Afrikaans term for separateness; the South African government's official race policy of ethnic separation in place from 1948 until 1990.

baas Boss; term used by South African blacks when addressing whites.

Black Consciousness Movement (BCM) South African antiapartheid activist movement formed in the 1960s that worked to cultivate pride in a cultural identity for blacks.

Black Economic Empowerment (BEE) Also known as Broad-Based Black Economic Empowerment (BBBEE); South African government policy intended to advance economic transformation and improve black economic participation in the nation's economy.

Black Sash Nonviolent antiapartheid white women's organization founded in South Africa in 1955.

Bophuthatswana Bantustan, or homeland, in northern South Africa declared independent in 1977.

Ciskei Bantustan, or homeland, in South Africa's Eastern Cape declared independent in 1981.

coloured Term used in South Africa for persons of mixed native and other blood.

Congress of South African Trade Unions (COSATU) South African antiapartheid trade union federation formed in 1985 and dedicated to a nonracial, nonsexist, democratic South Africa.

Eminent Persons Group (EPG) Committee of inquiry sent to South Africa in 1986 by the Commonwealth nations to determine if sanctions should be imposed.

Frontline States Organization formed in 1976 by five sub-Saharan African nations with the objective of ending colonialism and racism in southern Africa.

homelands Areas of land in South Africa designated to house specific ethnic groups; also called bantustans; known previously as reserves.

kaffir Derogatory term used by South African whites for a black South African.

National Party South African political party dedicated to apartheid, founded in 1914, which governed South Africa from 1948–1994.

Nats National Party members.

Pan Africanist Congress (PAC) Major black African political movement.

pass laws Series of laws designed to control the movement of Africans under apartheid.

Rivonia Trial Trial that took place in South Africa between 1963 and 1964 in which ten leaders of the African National Congress, including Nelson Mandela, were tried for acts of sabotage and conspiracy designed to overthrow the apartheid system.

Robben Island Island in Table Bay reestablished in 1961 as a prison for political prisoners, the majority of whom were black antiapartheid activists.

separate development A primary policy of apartheid starting in 1957 whereby historically black settled areas in South Africa were designated as "black homelands."

Sullivan Code Code of conduct for human rights and equal opportunity for companies operating in South Africa developed in 1977 by Reverend Leon Sullivan.

temporary sojourners Term used during the apartheid era for black Africans living in "white" South Africa.

TOT system South African system of paying farm workers part of their wages in wine.

Transkei South African bantustan along the Indian Ocean created by the South African government in 1959 and made a nominally independent homeland in 1976.

Tricameral Constitution of 1983 South African constitution that established a new structure of parliament—a tricameral parliament made up of a House of Assembly for whites, a House of Representatives for coloureds, and a House of Delegates for Indians (Asians), each of which determined laws relating to its racial group.

Truth and Reconciliation Commission (TRC) A court-like body established by the South African government in 1995 to help deal with what happened under apartheid and bring about a reconciliation of its people.

Umkhonto we Sizwe Spear of the Nation; military wing of the African National Congress founded in 1961.

United Democratic Front (UDF) An alliance formed in 1983 of more than six hundred organized antiapartheid protest groups.

Venda Homeland created for the Venda-speaking people in 1962, granted internal self-government in 1973, and granted full "independence" from South Africa in 1979.

Organizations to Contact

The editors have compiled the following list of organizations concerned with the issues debated in this book. The descriptions are derived from materials provided by the organizations. All have publications or information available for interested readers. The list was compiled on the date of publication of the present volume; the information provided here may change. Be aware that many organizations take several weeks or longer to respond to inquiries, so allow as much time as possible.

Amnesty International
5 Penn Plaza, 14th Floor
New York, NY, 10001
(212) 807-8400 • fax: (212) 463-9193
email: aimember@aiusa.org
website: www.amnestyusa.org

Amnesty International is a worldwide movement of people who campaign for internationally recognized human rights. Its vision is of a world in which every person enjoys all of the human rights enshrined in the Universal Declaration of Human Rights and other international human rights standards. Each year it publishes a report on its work and its concerns throughout the world.

Human Rights Institute of South Africa (HURISA)
4th Floor Elephant House, 105 Market Street
Johannesburg, South Africa
011 333 1730 • fax: 011 333 1735
website: hurisa.org.za

HURISA is a nonprofit nongovernmental organization that provides professional services toward the promotion of a human rights culture, peace, and democracy. It offers human rights training and education, distributes human rights information, and conducts research and advocacy. Its website contains links to information about its projects, research, training activities, and advocacy efforts, as well as to reports and other publications.

Human Rights Watch
350 Fifth Avenue, 34th Floor
New York, NY 10118-3299
(212) 290-4700 • (212) 736-1300
email: hrwnyc@hrw.org
website: www.hrw.org

Founded in 1978, this nongovernmental organization conducts systematic investigations of human rights abuses in countries around the world. It opposes discrimination against those with HIV/AIDS. It publishes many books and reports on specific countries and issues as well as annual reports and other articles. Its website includes numerous discussions of human rights and international justice issues.

International Crisis Group
420 Lexington Avenue, Suite 2640
New York, NY 10170
(212) 813-0820 • fax: (212) 813-0825
email: newyork@crisisgroup.org
website: www.crisisgroup.org

International Crisis Group is a Belgium-based nongovernmental organization committed to preventing and resolving deadly conflict. It is recognized as a leading independent, nonpartisan source of analysis and advice to governments and intergovernmental bodies on the prevention and resolution of deadly conflict. Its publications include *CrisisWatch*, a bulletin that assesses on a monthly basis the current status of approximately seventy countries, or areas of actual or potential conflict, and produces more than eighty reports and briefing papers annually.

**Montreal Institute for Genocide and Human Rights
Studies (MIGS)**
Concordia University
1455 De Maisonneuve Boulevard West
Montreal, Quebec, H3G 1M8 Canada
(514) 848-2424 ext. 5729 or 2404 • fax: (514) 848-4538
website: http://migs.concordia.ca

MIGS, founded in 1986, monitors native language media for early warning signs of genocide in countries deemed to be at risk of mass atrocities. The institute houses the Will to Intervene (W2I) Project, a research initiative focused on the prevention of genocide and other mass atrocity crimes. The institute also collects and disseminates research on the historical origins of mass killings and provides comprehensive links to this and other research materials on its website. The website also provides numerous links to other websites focused on genocide and related issues, as well as specialized sites organized by nation, region, or case.

**Office of the United Nations High Commissioner for Human
Rights (OHCHR)**
Palais Wilson, 52 rue des Pâquis
CH-1201 Geneva, Switzerland
41 22 917 9220
email: InfoDesk@ohchr.org
website: www.ohchr.org

The OHCHR works for the protection of human rights for all people, helps empower people to realize their rights, and assists those responsible for upholding such rights. It supports the work of the United Nations human rights mechanisms, such as the Human Rights Council, and works to ensure the enforcement of universally recognized human rights norms. Its publications include numerous brochures, handbooks, booklets, fact sheets, reference materials, training and educational materials, and special issue papers. Its website provides links to news articles, press releases, videos, speeches, and op-eds.

South African Human Rights Commission (SAHRC)
Braampark Forum 3, 33 Hoofd Street
Braamfontein, South Africa
011 877 3600
email: info@sahrc.org.za
website: www.sahrc.org.za

The SAHRC is an independent national human rights institution created to support constitutional democracy. It promotes, protects, monitors, and assesses the attainment and observance of human rights in South Africa. Its publications include newsletters, reports, pamphlets, and booklets. Its website provides links to a number of its publications as well as to relevant newspaper articles.

STAND
PO Box 26046
Washington, DC 20001
(202) 643-7238
email: info@standnow.org
website: www.standnow.org

STAND is a grassroots-based national student-led organization dedicated to the prevention of mass atrocities. STAND envisions a world in which the global community is willing and able to protect civilians from genocide and mass atrocities. In order to empower individuals and communities with the tools to prevent and stop genocide, STAND recommends activities from engaging government representatives to hosting fundraisers and has more than one thousand student chapters at colleges and high schools. While maintaining many documents online regarding genocide, STAND provides a plan to promote action as well as education.

United Human Rights Council (UHRC)
104 N. Belmont Street, Suite 313
Glendale, CA 91206
(818) 507-1933 • fax: (818) 240-3442
email: contact@uhrc.org
website: www.unitedhumanrights.org

The UHRC works toward exposing and correcting human rights violations of governments worldwide. It advances its goals and raises global awareness through grassroots mobilization, boycotts, community outreach, and education. Its website, which focuses on twentieth-century genocides, includes links to posts, photos, and videos.

List of Primary Source Documents

The editors have compiled the following list of documents that either broadly address genocide and persecution or more narrowly focus on the topic of this volume. The full text of these documents is available from multiple sources in print and online.

African Charter on Human and Peoples Rights

This 1981 charter is a declaration of human rights produced by the Organization of African Unity (OAU). Meant to encourage and protect human rights and basic freedoms in the African continent, it promotes and provides for a human rights commission and establishes the concept of "peoples" rights, as well as civil, political, economic, social, and cultural rights.

Annual Report: South Africa 2011

This report, issued by Amnesty International, addresses the prevailing status of human rights in South Africa. It provides background and identifies incidents within seven different human rights-related categories, including torture and other ill-treatment; violence against women and girls; and rights of lesbian, gay, bisexual, and transgender people.

Convention Against Torture and Other Cruel, Inhuman, or Degrading Punishment, United Nations, 1974

A draft resolution adopted by the United Nations General Assembly in 1974 opposing any nation's use of torture, unusually harsh punishment, and unfair imprisonment.

Convention on the Prevention and Punishment of the Crime of Genocide, December 9, 1948

A resolution of the United Nations General Assembly that defines genocide in legal terms and advises participating countries to prevent and punish actions of genocide in war and peacetime.

Harare Declaration, 1989

This document, which received international acceptance by such groups as the OAU Ad-Hoc Committee on Southern Africa, is an African National Congress statement of principles for a united, democratic, and nonracial state. It also deals with the climate for and process of negotiations to bring about such a state and details actions to be taken.

Human Rights Report: South Africa, 2011

This report issued by the United States Department of State addresses the prevailing status of human rights in South Africa and identifies specific incidents within seven different human rights-related categories, including respect for the integrity of the person, respect for civil liberties, and respect for political rights.

International Convention on the Suppression and Punishment of the Crime of Apartheid, 1976

A resolution of the United Nations General Assembly that declares that apartheid is a crime against humanity and that "inhuman acts resulting from the policies and practices of apartheid and similar policies and practices of racial segregation and discrimination" are international crimes.

Principles of International Law Recognized in the Charter of the Nuremburg Tribunal, United Nations International Law Commission, 1950

After World War II (1939–1945) the victorious allies legally tried surviving leaders of Nazi Germany in the German city of Nuremburg. The proceedings established standards for international law that were affirmed by the United Nations and by later court tests. Among other standards, national leaders can be held responsible for crimes against humanity, which might include "murder, extermination, deportation, enslavement, and other inhuman acts."

Rome Statute of the International Criminal Court, July 17, 1998

The treaty that established the International Criminal Court. It establishes the court's functions, jurisdiction, and structure.

Truth and Reconciliation Commission of South Africa Report

This epic seven-volume report—the first five volumes issued in 1998 and the final two in 2003—chronicles South Africa's apartheid history from 1960–1994. Each volume has a particular focus, ranging from the commission of gross violations of human rights to the commission's conclusions and recommendations. The report serves as a record of the hearings that exposed human rights violations committed by the South African government and conflicting parties.

United Nations General Assembly Resolution 96 on the Crime of Genocide, December 11, 1946

A resolution of the United Nations General Assembly that affirms that genocide is a crime under international law.

Universal Declaration of Human Rights United Nations, 1948

Soon after its founding, the United Nations approved this general statement of individual rights it hoped would apply to citizens of all nations.

Whitaker Report on Genocide, 1985

This report addresses the question of the prevention and punishment of the crime of genocide. It calls for the establishment of an international criminal court and a system of universal jurisdiction to ensure that genocide is punished.

For Further Research

Books

David Beresford, *Truth Is a Strange Fruit: A Personal Journey Through the Apartheid War.* Johannesburg, South Africa: Jacana Media, 2011.

Kenneth S. Broun, *Saving Nelson Mandela: The Rivonia Trial and the Fate of South Africa.* Oxford, England: Oxford University Press, 2012.

Nancy L. Clark and William H. Worger, *South Africa: The Rise and Fall of Apartheid.* London: Pearson Education Limited, 2011.

Geoffrey V. Davis, *Voices of Justice and Reason: Apartheid and Beyond in South African Literature.* Amsterdam, The Netherlands: Rodopi, 2003.

F.W. de Klerk, *The Last Trek—A New Beginning: The Autobiography.* New York: St. Martin's Press, 1999.

David Downing, *Apartheid in South Africa.* Chicago: Heinemann Library, 2004.

Jillian Edelstein, *Truth and Lies: Stories from the Truth and Reconciliation Commission in South Africa.* New York: The New Press, 2002.

William Finnegan, *Crossing the Line: A Year in the Land of Apartheid.* Berkeley and Los Angeles, CA: University of California Press, 1994.

Philip Frankel, *An Ordinary Atrocity: Sharpeville and Its Massacre.* New Haven, CT: Yale University Press, 2001.

Philip Hummel, *My Life Growing up White During Apartheid in South Africa.* Bloomington, IN: AuthorHouse, 2011.

Joel Joffe, *The State vs. Nelson Mandela: The Trial That Changed South Africa.* Oxford, England: Oneworld Publications, 2007.

Colin and Margaret Legum, *South Africa: Crisis for the West.* New York: Praeger, 1964.

Tom Lodge, *Sharpeville: an Apartheid Massacre and Its Consequences.* New York: Oxford University Press, 2011.

Mac Maharaj and Ahmed Kathrada (editorial consultants), *Mandela: The Authorized Portrait.* Kansas City, MO: Andrews McMeel Publishing, 2006.

Miriam Mathabane (as told to Mark Mathabane), *Miriam's Song.* New York: Simon & Schuster, 2000.

Godfrey Mwakikagile, *Africa 1960–1970: Chronicle and Analysis.* Tanzania: New Africa Press, 2009.

Padraig O'Malley, *Shades of Difference: Mac Maharaj and the Struggle for South Africa.* New York: Viking Penguin, 2007.

David B. Ottaway, *Chained Together: Mandela, De Klerk, and the Struggle to Remake South Africa.* New York: Times Books, 1993.

Lynda Schuster, *A Burning Hunger: One Family's Struggle Against Apartheid.* Athens, OH: Ohio University Press, 2004.

David Welch, *The Rise and Fall of Apartheid.* Johannesburg and Cape Town, South Africa: Jonathan Ball Publishers, 2009.

Periodicals and Internet Sources

Associated Press, "U.S. Leads List with 134 Companies Pulling Out: 188 Firms Have Left South Africa, Survey Finds," *Los Angeles Times*, May 31, 1988. http://articles.latimes.com.

Tahar Ben Jelloun, "Nelson Mandela: A Giant of Our Time," *Unesco Courier*, November 1995. http://unesdoc.unesco.org.

James Cason, Lisa Crooms, and Jennifer Davis, "Questions and Answers on Divestment," *South Africa Perspectives*, July 1987.

"Colour Me South African: Learning to Live in a Rainbow Society," *The Economist*, June 3, 2010. www.economist.com.

Economist Special Correspondent, "One Sane Country," *The Economist*, May 27, 1961.

Alexandra Fuller, "Mandela's Children," *National Geographic*, June 2010.

Nadine Gordimer, "Apartheid, the 'Agitator,'" *New York Times*, June 27, 1976. www.nytimes.com.

Paul Gray, James R. Gaines, Joelle Attinger, Nelson Mandela, and F.W. de Klerk, "Nelson Mandela and F.W. de Klerk," *Time*, November 3, 2005. www.time.com.

Scott Kraft, "Apartheid Foes Stage Huge Rally," *Los Angeles Times*, October 30, 1989.

Lance Morrow, "Birth of a Nation," *Time*, May 9, 1994.

Alan Paton, "The South African Treason Trial," *The Atlantic*, January 1960.

Lydia Polgreen, "In a Divided City, Many Blacks See Echoes of White Superiority," *New York Times*, March 22, 2012.

Jack Reed, "Grayed but Unbowed, Mandela Is Freed," UPI Stories. http://100years.upi.com.

James Robbins, "The Mandela Moment That Changed South Africa," BBC News, February 10, 2010. www.news.bbc.co.uk.

Randall Robinson, "We Lost—and De Klerk Won," *Newsweek*, July 29, 1991. www.thedailybeast.com/newsweek.

Leslie Rubin, "South Africa Facts and Fiction," *Unesco Courier*, November 1977. http://unesdoc.unesco.org.

Alex Duval Smith, "Why FW de Klerk Let Nelson Mandela out of Prison," *The Observer*, January 30, 2010. www.guardian .co.uk.

David Smith, "Ghosts of South African Prison Tell What Apartheid Really Meant," *The Guardian*, December 31, 2009. www.guardian.co.uk.

Richard Stengel, "Nelson Mandela: The Making of a Leader," *Time*, May 9, 1994.

Truth and Reconciliation Commission, "The TRC Final Report," www.justice.gov.za.

Humphrey Tyler, "White S. African Researchers Blast Apartheid Policy," *Christian Science Monitor*, July 8, 1985. www.cs monitor.com.

Erik Van Ees, "2 Riots, 2 Years and Too Much Bloodshed," *Chicago Tribune*, September 7, 1986. http://articles.chicago tribune.com.

Websites

African National Congress (www.anc.org.za). This website contains a wealth of information about South Africa, past and present, including links to a large collection of historic documents, speeches, reports, and books as well as biographical information about ANC leaders.

Allafrica.com:South Africa (www.allafrica.com/south africa). This website provides documents and resources; news reports and headlines from African and worldwide sources; and information about various topics, including human rights.

Apartheid in South Africa: Living Under Racial Segregation and Discrimination (www.bbc.co.uk/archive/apartheid). This BBC archive collection focuses on the life of the average South African under apartheid and key moments in the antiapartheid struggle as expressed in twenty-two programs originally broadcast between 1954 and 1996 and eight key documents written between 1957 and 1986.

The Heart of Hope: South Africa's Transition from Apartheid to Democracy (www.nelsonmandela.org/omalley). This website contains interviews with key people who influenced South African political history, chronologies of events, demographic and economy-related data, key historical documents, charters and treaties, hearing transcripts, reports, racial legislation, and much more.

Mandela: An Audio History (www.radiodiaries.org/mandela /mstories.html). This website consists of an award-winning series of radio diaries, complete with transcripts, which, in five segments offer first-person accounts of the antiapartheid struggle. The website also includes an audio timeline of six decades in the life of Nelson Mandela and the history of apartheid.

South Africa: Overcoming Apartheid, Building Democracy (www.overcomingapartheid.msu.edu/index.php). This website features video and audio interviews with South African activists, eight chronological narrative units that cover the history of South African apartheid, in-depth essays that incorporate multimedia material and links to other primary materials, and an extensive media collection on key events in the antiapartheid struggle with links to corresponding web images and documents.

South African History Online (www.sahistory.org.za). This website contains a large collection of biographies, timelines, online books, and photo galleries.

Southern African Freedom Struggles, 1950–1994 (www.disa .ukzn.ac.za/index.php?option=com_content&view=article& id=47&Itemid = 55). This page of the Digital Imaging South Africa (DISA) website offers an alphabetized list of links to full-text articles, essays, interviews, paintings, photographs, oral histories, and more—all related to the antiapartheid struggle.

Film and Video

Amandla!: A Revolution in Four-Part Harmony (2002). This documentary tells the story of protest music in South Africa and the role it played in the struggle against apartheid.

Cry Freedom (1987). This feature film, based on the true story of the friendship of South African journalist Donald Woods and black activist Steve Biko, deals with Woods's investigation of Biko's suspicious death and Woods's flight from South Africa as a result of his investigation.

Cry, the Beloved Country (1995). This feature film tells the story of two fathers whose lives collide in the 1940s in apartheid South Africa, one a black Anglican priest from a rural town whose son has killed the son of the other, a wealthy white landowner.

Mandela and de Klerk (1997). This television film tells Nelson Mandela's story of his twenty-seven-year struggle to bring an end to apartheid and the role played by South African president F.W. de Klerk in helping Mandela achieve his goal.

The World Witnesses the Soweto Uprising (http://video.pbs.org /video/2185498596). This video includes actual footage of the 1976 student uprising in South Africa's Soweto township accompanied by explanatory narratives by black South Africans.

Index